HOW MY WIFE AND I TEAMED UP TO BECOME MILLIONAIRES IN FIVE YEARS

A Universal System of Land Transactions
by Jim Stephenson

Copyright© 1977 by Jim Stephenson, and all rights are reserved.

No part of this book may be duplicated or reproduced in any form or method except with the expressed written permission of Jim Stephenson.

Third Printing, September 1977

Dedication

This book is dedicated to my good friend and Certified Public Accountant — Neal Elden and his beloved wife June.

Neal has been with me since the time I developed a net worth of about $35,000. He has given me excellent financial advice, but he's also given me something that is even more important.

He has taught me that there is more to money than the pursuit of it and that there is more to life than money.

Meet The Stephensons

Jim and Dianne Stephenson

Jim and Dianne Stephenson took a $500 loan and turned it into a $1,000,000 profit in less than five years. By emphasizing a team approach to their business they were able to use a limited number of outside advisors to accomplish a professional job. They kept profits high and capital outlay low. Stephenson Enterprises has now become so successful that nationwide expansion is underway.

By developing, perfecting—and using—their universal land transaction system, the Stephensons were able to enjoy early semiretirement after only five years. During this period, they made many improvements to their ranch. Jim went lake trout fishing and deer hunting, while Dianne cultivated beautiful and bountiful vegetable gardens.

While traveling to new and exciting places, the Stephensons discovered that they really enjoyed meeting new people and making new friends. They decided to reenter their business operation on a full-time scale because they wanted to "get back to work" and because they are looking forward to meeting their readers. They expect that many profitable partnership arrangements will be developed as a direct result of this book and they can't wait to get started on what they expect to be the most exciting time of their lives.

The Stephensons hold membership in many civic and business organizations and devote time to these groups.

Reader's Note

The thesis of this book is to explain how Jim Stephenson developed his financial security and became successful by using a particular system of purchasing and selling land.

Jim Stephenson, the author, is not an attorney, a CPA, or an accountant. He does not claim to be an expert, in any of these professions. Although he has no formal education beyond the 8th Grade, Jim Stephenson was able to become financially secure by following the guides he presents in this book, a volume that can correctly be called "the how-to guide to financial success and security."

The suggestions in this book are based upon his actual experience in land transactions. They are meant to serve as a guide to those who are interested in attempting to duplicate his methods. Several actual transactions are noted. They should not be construed by the reader as particular advice on any given piece of property with which the reader may want to become involved.

The book is a guideline—a blueprint—of how one man made money in the land business. The author believes the blueprint has universal application for his readers.

Third Printing
September 1977

Table of Contents

Reader's Note	6
Advice to Readers	9
Prologue	11
Introduction	15
I'm Glad to Meet You	19
The Universal System of Land Transactions	25
I'm in the Land Business	31
Five Basic Lessons	37
The Key	43
A Family Approach	47
Beginning the Venture	53
Get Familiar With Your Home County	59
Our First Deal	65
Nagging Questions	71
Meet My CPA	75
More Deals, More Profits	81
Accumulate Your Wealth	87
The Big Deal Will Come	93
More Sophisticated Transactions	99
We Make the Headlines	105
A New Avenue to Leads and Contacts	111
Every Texan Has a Gas Well— So I Got One, Too!	117
One Deal Leads to Another	121
A Very Personal Deal	125
A Bad Deal Turns Good	129
Settling Down on the Ranch	133
I'll Be Your Partner	139
Interest Table	143

A UNIVERSAL SYSTEM OF LAND TRANSACTIONS
Marinella Haygood

Advice to Readers

POSITIVE MENTAL ATTITUDE

Don't begin reading this book until you are sure you will have an opportunity to do so without unnecessary interference. There is always a tendency to read through "how-to" books quickly, but try to avoid it in this case. It may take a couple of sittings and an ample period of time to give the ideas contained herein their deserved attention.

Not because the book is complicated—it's not. But because it is an important book. It is important because it may very well play a key role in determining the financial condition of your future.

Go to the den. Go to the bedroom. Go to the library. Go somewhere quiet so that you can give these ideas your complete consideration. If you are to become successful, you must learn to think clearly about what you are doing. Give the task at hand your complete attention. It will save you costly mistakes and time-consuming corrections in the future.

The fact that you have ordered this book indicates that, at this point, you do not have the level of financial success and security that you want. People who already have enough money to take care of their wants and needs don't order books telling them how to make more money by some special method.

You must think positively about what you are doing. When you *truly* believe that you will succeed at the task you have assigned yourself, you will be amazed at what you will actually be able to accomplish. Financial security will become a reality. I don't mean to imply that there won't be some work involved—there will be. But a good positive mental attitude makes the work much easier and having confidence in what you are setting out to do is essential to getting the most out of your efforts.

But take heart. The fact that you have ordered this book does indicate that you have the courage to think positively. Begin right now to think that you *will* succeed. Just because you may have failed in the past doesn't mean that this system won't work for you. In fact, I know that this system can do everything I have promised. But you have to use it correctly.

Positive thinking is also important from another point. It allows your creativity to escape. Because the system that I'm going to describe is a universal system—in other words, it is a system that applies to all types of land transactions—a positive, creative approach to the book will enable you to see ways that you can personally apply the system to your own geographic location, your own style of living, your own strong points, and other things that make you and your situation different from every other person and situation in the world. You may see ways to use this system that others, including myself, have not yet seen. Remember that this book is a guide. It is not a law. Adapt your thinking and your individual character to this book. It will work successfully just the way I have described, but this does not mean that you can't take my idea and improve it to serve your own needs.

Be analytical later. Right now, be receptive so that you can get the enthusiasm that you will need—the positive thinking that success demands—to become successful.

At the end of each chapter, the book will leave space for The Reader's Page. Take advantage of the space provided to develop ideas you may form while reading each section. If you have questions, use this space to jot them down and answer them. Make other notes that you find useful. You may also want to outline thoughts for later reference. Use this space to help you remember what you have read and to determine how your new knowledge will help you most in your goal to achieve financial success and security.

You will succeed!!

Prologue

My name is Dr. Bill Shaw. I am a professional man—a veterinarian to be exact. I have an established practice in the metropolitan area.

Most people expect professsional men to be financially secure, particularly doctors of any specialty. If I told you that my financial statement makes many people envious, you probably wouldn't be too surprised. In fact, this is the case.

Have you ever wondered why so many professional men and women become financially secure? It's not because we have better or greater knowledge about how to make money. We don't. It *is* because professional people have learned the necessity of depending upon other professionals—or knowledgeable people—in the field of investments.

Consider this example.

If your pet needs medical attention, will you take it to a lawyer, a plumber, an electrician, a carpenter, a painter, or a journalist? Certainly not. The obvious answer to the question is to take the animal to a veterinarian—a professional man or woman whose training has prepared him to immediately identify what is wrong with your pet. After he has identified the problem, he has the knowledge to prescribe treatment to restore good health to the animal. By consulting the professional, you have saved your pet from an annoying problem, such as fleas; a serious illness, such as pneumonia; or even possible death. The veterinarian has the ability to diagnose and treat minor ailments as well as emergency afflictions. The key word is *expertise*. The professional must be able to find the problem and treat it correctly and quickly.

My medical school prepared me to treat animals. It did not prepare me to invest money.

But just as you seek out the veterinarian when your pet is ill, I know to consult knowledgeable people when I want to invest money or make a financial deal. I learned this lesson early, but it took some time before I found the method of investing that worked best for me.

I tried many avenues. I invested money in the stock market—and lost. I bought all types of commodities—with little success. Although none of these setbacks destroyed me, I quickly learned that these types of investments—even under the direction of top-notch stockbrokers and commodity experts—don't always work. And some are risky.

I can truthfully state that I did not have any greatly successful investments until I became friends with Jim Stephenson.

The first time I met Jim was the day he brought his dog to my clinic for treatment. Although we had never met before, I was immediately impressed with him. After talking with him for a few minutes, I felt that I had known him a lifetime. We became good friends and our friendship has endured throughout the years.

As our friendship grew, we had more personal discussions. I soon told him of my attempts to make rewarding investments in the stock market and commodities. At that time, he told me how he had made substantial money in buying and selling land. In a very real sense, he led me and my investment group through our first land transaction which grossed a profit of over $20,000. Another transaction that Jim carefully directed brought us an additional $100,000.

Since then, I have been on my own in investments. Because of these investments, today I am partial owner in a highly successful emergency animal clinic in the greater Houston area. I also own a very profitable sporting goods store.

My expertise in investing was developed because of my close association with Jim. I am not saying that I might never have increased my financial assets without him. But I can definitely say that without him I might still be trying.

I began this introduction by discussing why professional men and women are often financially secure. It is the respect we have for our own profession that teaches us to respect the expertise necessary in other fields.

Jim Stephenson is a financial professional. I respect him, and I am proud to introduce him to you.

Introduction

Clyde Godbold is a banker with over 30 years experience in lending, marketing, public relations and special projects.

Jim and Dianne Stephenson have been my personal friends for many years. It gives me a great deal of pleasure to introduce them to you.

This book will tell you their amazing success story, a story I witnessed and found truly astonishing.

Because I have been in the banking business for over 30 years, I have had the opportunity to watch many people improve their financial conditions. I have seen middle-class people become moderately wealthy. I've seen wealthy people add to their fortunes. And I've seen a few people start with literally nothing and make large amounts of money.

But the book you are about to read tells the most amazing transformation in financial conditions I've ever seen in my banking career. If I had to isolate one success story as being the most outstanding of all the successes I've seen throughout the years, this unique story is the one I would select.

I'm especially proud to have this opportunity to tell you about Jim and Dianne Stephenson.

I first met Jim in the mid-1950's. At that time, he was a young man whose ambition was to make a successful and honest living as a salesman. I found this somewhat amusing as it isn't too often that you hear of a star salesman with a speech impediment!

But Jim had a great deal of confidence in himself and the fact that he might be at a disadvantage in his chosen field because of his stuttering apparently didn't bother him. At any rate, his enthusiasm and optimism about his ability to sell vacuum cleaners door-to-door successfully was never dampened.

During the next several years, Jim periodically borrowed $50 or $100 to keep from starving to death. It didn't look like vacuum cleaners would lead him to the financial success and security he wanted.

One evening he came to me with a new idea. He was extremely excited about this plan—so excited, in fact, that it was several minutes before I could understand the words "sewing machines." The salesman in Jim believed that there was great financial opportunity in this product. He asked for $300 to put his new plan into action. I believed in Jim and was confident that he would repay it. But I was really surprised when he repaid the total loan in only four days!

I confess that I never expected Jim to find great success in this venture, although he had persuaded me to buy one. To this day, I have no idea of the exact success that Jim had selling sewing machines, but it was at this point that I stopped being amused and began to take him very seriously.

I continued to see Jim in a business capacity so I wasn't too surprised when he stopped by my bank one evening about 15 years ago. As it turned out, that visit was strictly social. Jim told me that he was getting married. We celebrated over a bottle of *Pepsi*. Soon afterwards, Jim and the charming Dianne married. Dianne was exactly the type of woman that Jim needed to help him realize his ambitions. He put aside any fears of failure and with a great deal of courage, faith, determination—and skill—overcame his seemingly insurmountable obstacles to attain his goal of financial success and security. Together they turned his dream into reality.

One of the first projects they undertook was buying an apartment in a rather depressed area of Houston. They remodeled it and added on a couple of efficiencies. This sparked their idea to buy and sell modest houses and apartments. I extended them secured and unsecured loans in moderate amounts from time to time. As it later turned out, this was their first step in attaining success and security.

Soon after they began this project, they conceived the idea of buying land at a cost below its market value and reselling it for a comfortable profit. As you will learn, this scheme resulted in their becoming millionaires in about five years.

Jim and Dianne Stephenson now live in a beautiful home in suburban Houston. Their house and furnishings are easily worth over a quarter million dollars and they own a ranch worth at least a million dollars. The financial statement they boast is impressive in both capital and holdings. Without question, Jim and Dianne are very successful.

When I think back, I'm still amused about the small loans Jim made to "keep the wolves from the door." I hope their story will be as inspirational to you as it has been to me and the many others who know them.

Clyde G. Godbold

If that is all there is, what is it worth?

(Handwritten annotation at top: GOD, will Provide. GOD's WILL should ALWAYS BE YOUR FIRST PRIORITY)

Chapter One
I'm Glad To Meet You

You have read a lot about me but you haven't actually met me yet. My name is Jim Stephenson, and I'm glad to meet you.

From the advertisement that convinced you to buy this book, you discovered that I was successful and financially secure. You also found out that my success and security were the result of buying and selling land.

I have a system of buying and selling land that, if duplicated by you, can make you financially secure. You know that I did not finish high school and that I am not an accountant or a lawyer. In fact I have no formal training in any profession. And yet, I still claim to have a method that gave me financial security and success and I am stating that it will work for you.

I've never met you, and I don't know your name. But, believe it or not, I already know a little bit about you too.

I know that there is a good chance that you are having money problems. Possibly they are not outright problems, but I think it would be safe to say that you are not totally satisfied with the amount of money you have to spend on a day-to-day, month-to-month, or year-to-year basis. People with a great deal of money do not generally respond to advertisements which tell them how to make more money by some special method.

You wrote because you see the need for additional financial assets and you think that I can help you. I believe that I can help you too. In a very real sense, then, we are partners.

As partners with a common background— you have little money now and I had very little money when I began— I am going to tell you my personal story.

But before I do, and because I am what I am—after all, partners must understand each other—you are going to have to listen to some of my moralizing before we get down to the "nuts and bolts" of land business.

The dedication of this book is more than just words to me. It has real meaning because of my deep respect for my CPA, Neal Elden.

He has taught me there is more to money than the pursuit of it and that there is more to life than money.

Neal once told me a story which dramatically illustrates the meaning of money. He said, "Imagine yourself as the only person in the world. Then imagine yourself transported to New York City, the world's financial capital.

"Walk down the street where the richest banks in the whole world line the sidewalks. All the banks' vaults are open to you. Go in. They are filled with fresh currency, yours for the taking.

"Take all the money you can carry out. Come back and get some more if you want.

"But now, come back to reality. When you leave that bank with all of the money that you want, you're the richest man in the world. But just remember, you are the *only* man in the world.

"And then what in God's name is all of that money good for?"

What did the wealth of Howard Hughes give him? Isolation and despair. What legacy did his money leave? A dozen or more forged wills and humans gouging for every possible penny they can get their hands on— whether they deserve it or not.

This book will tell you how to make money. I firmly believe that. But I also feel morally obligated to get you thinking of money in more than one way. I want to get you thinking about yourself.

The Reader's Page at the end of this chapter will give you an opportunity to participate in what I believe is an essential exercise in self-identity. You and your family make lists of those things which are important to

A Means to an End — to

[handwritten margin notes: Help others — To Achieve Freedom — Help Usher God's Kingdom — A Better World Tomorrow For All]

you. Everyone should make a separate list. You might include such things as strong religious beliefs, good health, nice possessions, financial security, property, intelligent children, a new car, a new dishwasher—everything that you need or that you would like to have. This may take some time because you should give this list your full thought.

Once the list is completed, the hard part begins.

Take your list and arrange the items according to the priority in which you want to accomplish them. Now take all the lists and compare them.

Don't be ashamed if financial security is one of the top items on most of the lists. There is nothing inherently evil about wealth.

Money has produced cures to diseases. It has provided for the poor. It has built great universities and added to man's knowledge. It has accomplished many humanitarian goals.

But wealth has also distorted the values of many who have obtained it. This is why it is important for you and your family to define your goals now. Describe your values and know who you are. Save this list as a reminder of who you were and what you were before you became financially independent. Financial success and security lie before you. But don't ever forget how you began.

Always regard money as a tool, not as a god. If the pursuit of money becomes your God, then you will become money's Satan.

Readers Comments

Dear Mr. & Mrs. Stephenson,
 I have just finished reading your book. It is indeed one of the best books I have ever read. I have always been a positive thinking person, always trying to come up with ideas on making money.
 After reading your book, I can see just where I have failed. What I needed was a guide.
  Mr. Poovelt, New Orleans, Louisiana

The Reader's Page

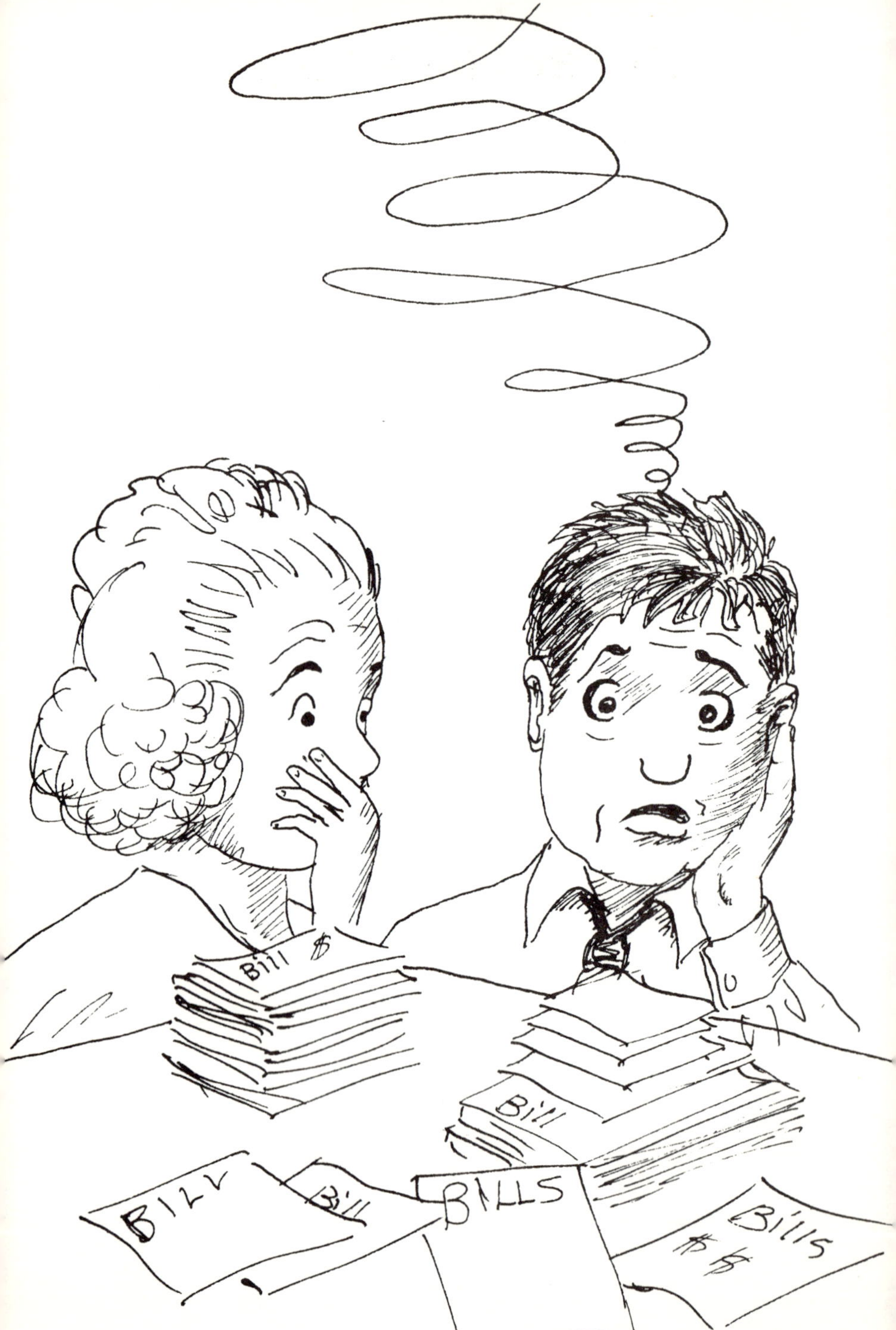
Bill
Bill
Bill
BILLS
Bills

Chapter Two
The Universal System Of Land Transactions

I must admit that I have done a lot of reading in preparation for writing this book. Of course, I was already familiar with all aspects of the sytem of buying and selling land which I have used to become financially secure—a millionaire in fact.

But how should I go about explaining it? What should I write to convince you, the reader, that you can accomplish the same success?

Should I hire a writer to go out and research the lives of many great men who have made money in the past? Should I hire someone to read the biographies of Hughes, Hunt, the Rockefellers, Hearst, Kennedy and all the others who have achieved financial heights? I admit that I gave these ideas, as well as others, some consideration.

I have been told that psychologically everybody likes to think that he can duplicate the feats of the powerful and rich men of the world. Although they would certainly make interesting reading, biographies of rich men may not tell you *how* to make money.

My purpose in writing this book is not to entertain you. It is to tell you how to become successful and secure. Besides, the truth is that few will ever accumulate the massive wealth of the financial giants.

So I ruled out telling the stories of these famous people. That left me with only one alternative. I decided to tell you my story. I think that it is a story which may have more relevance to you than the stories of the "giants" anyway. It is something that you can read and then say to yourself, "If he did it, so can I." It will be easier for you to follow in my steps than to follow the steps of Hughes or Hearst.

Why? For one thing, I am probably a little like you. I had no professional background and I had no previous experience in the land business prior to this venture. I had "dabbled" a little bit in apartments, but that was the extent of my land dealing. And yet I became a sophisticated buyer and seller of land.

I dropped out of school in the 8th Grade. At the age of 16, I ran away from home and began working on a tugboat in the Houston ship channel. When I joined the Army at the age of 18, I was nothing more than a deck hand.

After spending several years in the service, I returned to Houston and began to sell vacuum cleaners. This started my career as a salesman. Through the years, I sold a variety of merchandise. Since my selling jobs never provided me with more than enough money for the necessities of life, I was always struggling to pay bills and provide for my family.

I use to think that my failure to gain financial success and security was a result of not having enough education. I don't feel that way any more. Many people who have made a good living and accomplished their goals did so without a great deal of formal education. Education is important, but so is having a specific goal in mind and working hard to achieve that goal. If a person is willing to concentrate his efforts and talents in acquiring his goal, then the lack of formal education can be overcome. Just think about the many well-educated people who are not successful and financially secure and you will see what I mean.

If I had felt that being well-educated was the most important factor in achieving success, I would have hired a college graduate who majored in economics to research and write this book. I would have had him include lengthy statistical tables and complicated economic charts to demonstrate his points. I would have made sure that he used long words and complex terms that only the very well-educated understand. I would have asked him to refer to economic theories that even economic experts might have trouble understanding.

But the point of this book is to make my system clear. I don't want to confuse you. I do want to impress upon you the fact that you can achieve success like I did. I'm certainly not familiar with difficult statistics, economics and complicated mathematics. And they are not important to my system. This is the reason I wrote the book myself. I will use language that anyone can understand, and if I use a term that you might not know, I will explain it.

The method I use is not complicated. That is why I call it a Universal System. The dictionary defines *universal* as something that is understood by everyone. It is a principle that allows action within broad limits. It is also something that is comprehensive and has wide application. This is important to you because something that is universal can be changed to meet the needs of those individuals who use it. This means that you can take my system and use it in a way that fits your own situation.

My personal background is modest, even humble. I am a simple man who probably couldn't have made a success of something that was difficult to understand and complicated to use. The sheer simplicity of my advice and easy explanation of this universal system of land transactions should inspire you to try this method of gaining financial success and security.

I hope it does.

Readers Comments

Jim,
*   I have your book and have read it from cover to cover many times. I do like what you say, and the way you say it. You speak my language. For the first time, I do believe I have found something that could work for me.*
*   Mr. Harvey Prather, Keltoneong, Ohio*

The Reader's Page

Try to reach higher means to achieve success in all areas of life

Help everybody as everybody has always helped you!

Be a-light to the world

From this promised country of bounty (the bountiful!)

FINANCIAL SECURITY

Chapter Three
I'm In The Land Business

We have all heard variations of that old saying, "The journey of a million miles begins with a single step." If I didn't qualify my use of that phrase, no doubt many of you would say, "Well, here comes the snow job."

But how trite would that phrase be to you personally if we substitute a million dollars for a million miles and your first step is to read and understand this book?

That cliché was trite to me too until I obtained the financial security that I wanted and that my family needed. When I look back now, it amazes me to realize just what small-time operators we were.

I vividly remember going to a party shortly after I had started in the land business and being asked by a rather distinguished gentlemen, "What do you do for a living?"

I answered, "I'm in the land business."

He asked me where I bought and sold land. This gentleman, himself very successful in another field, looked shocked when I told him, "Well, I haven't bought or sold any yet."

When I tell that story today, we all laugh. But it certainly brings back memories of the time when we hadn't made it.

You will never want to forget these times. It will help you to appreciate just what you have achieved after you become successful.

What was my first small step to financial success and security? It came in 1967. It was so simple that actually I am convinced it was complicated. In fact, it was so simple that I didn't even realize its meaning until several months later.

After it happened, I thought about it often. Something was nagging at me trying to tell me that something important to my future had just happened. Finally it struck home.

I will lay the circumstances before you. See if you can make the connections.

In 1967, a friend came to see me seeking advice. He owned 10 acres of land in a county adjacent to Harris County, the home of metropolitan Houston. However, the land he owned was in a rural county. Next to his property were 80 acres of land that he wanted to purchase.

The owner of the 80-acre tract lived out-of-state. My friend wrote him a letter explaining that he wanted to buy the land. In straightforward terms, he asked the owner to name a price at which he would be willing to sell. The owner's reply stated an offer to sell the tract at $750 per acre.

My friend was pleased. He felt certain that the value of the land was higher than the figure quoted. But he didn't know the next step to take in order to actually acquire it. I didn't know a whole lot more, but I outlined a course of action.

I suggested he put down $500 earnest money with a title company in his home town toward purchasing the property. (Earnest money is an amount of money that a buyer gives to a seller or his representative to bind a contract. It serves to end a bargain, although a transaction is not finalized until final payment is made. A title company is a firm specializing in land law and other real estate work. The attorneys who work for a title company are experts in the field of land transactions.)

The title company drew up an earnest money contract and sent it to the owner of the 80 acres. As it turned out, the owner accepted the contract, giving my friend the legal authority to initiate the process of finding a buyer for land that he was purchasing.

The next step my friend had to take was to sell the land. How did he go about it? He put an advertisement in a major Houston metropolitan newspaper. In several days, he had a buyer. The new selling price was fixed at $1,500 per acre.

When the transaction was completed, my friend had gained a profit of over $60,000!

The Reader's Page

Winston Churchill in 1922 when he said "...Land is the original source of all wealth..." and "Land monopoly is not the only monopoly, but it is by far the greatest of monopolies—it is a perpetual monopoly, and it is the mother of all forms of monopoly."

Land has always been one of the best investments for all economic seasons. Today, when inflation and taxes together are taking a heavy toll of most methods of wealth accumulation, land investments are more valuable than ever. Unlike bonds, savings accounts, life insurance, and similar "creditor" types of investment, land investment provides the opportunity to actually *profit by inflation*—and, in addition, it offers *big tax advantages* to boot.

DR. WILLIAM SHAW

The Reader's Page

LAND OWNERSHIP
— THE PRIME OWNERSHIP
(THE ORIGINAL MONOPOLY)
LAND APPRECIATION

- 1. SOME PEOPLE WANT TO SELL THEIR PROPERTY
- 2. IDENTIFY WHO WANTS TO SELL
- 3. YOU DON'T HAVE TO START BIG TO GET BIG.
- 4. GO TO A TITLE COMPANY
- 5. KNOW HOW TO SELL LAND

Chapter Four
Five Basic Lessons

There are many lessons to be learned from that story.

The first is that there are people who own property and want to sell it. They already have a definite idea of the amount they want or need to make the transaction final.

Property owners pay school, city, county, and state taxes. Generally speaking, they know the value of their property. (When you pay your school taxes this year, just see if you get an indication of the value of your property!)

This is an important lesson. It is the basis of my system. I will repeat it.

There are people who want to sell their property right now and they know how much money they need to finalize the transaction.

People need money for a variety of reasons. They may have medical bills. They may have four children in college. They may want to run for political office and need the cash. They may want to take a once-in-a-lifetime vacation. Think of all the people you know, and you will have at least that many different reasons why people want money.

One way to obtain a relatively large amount of money quickly is through the selling of property. This is the second lesson.

Identify who wants to sell their property.

The goal of your new business is to identify those people who want to sell their property and who know how much money it will take to finalize the transaction.

What is lesson three? It's a bit of philosophy I always keep in mind.

You don't have to start big to get big.

My friend made over $60,000 with an initial investment of only $500 for an earnest money contract and a small amount to run a classified ad in a newspaper. This minor investment brought my friend more money than he had ever had in his life.

The fourth lesson to be learned from the story is to *seek professional advice.*

My friend went to a title company at the beginning of his transaction. If you already have an attorney with whom you do business, consult him if you prefer. But do get legal advice. Try to make connections with a lawyer or a title company that can advise you throughout all of your business transactions. The lawyer will become familiar with your business and your preferences. He will be able to save you a great deal of time. Even more important, he will probably save you a great deal of money on a long-term basis.

What is the fifth lesson of this story?

Know how to sell land.

My friend bought land at a price that was below market value and he was able to sell it quickly at a profit. This is the type of transaction that is profitable for someone just beginning in the land business. By purchasing land that you can sell quickly and on which you can gain a profit, you will avoid having to hold land for long periods of time. Your money will be able to work quicker, as you will be freeing it rather than tying it up. Later in your business, you will probably want to hold some pieces of land, but this should be avoided in the begining unless you have ample funds to use.

When I first started, I didn't plan to make $50,000 or even close to that amount on my first deal. I certainly wanted to, if possible, but I would have settled for $10,000 or even a smaller profit. This still would have been more than I had before I started.

As it turned out, my first deal was for much more than $10,000. But I do urge you to exercise restraint in the beginning.

These basic lessons, plus intelligent caution and

restraint, are the principles I learned from my friend's transaction. He didn't know exactly what he had done or just why it worked. As I said, it took quite a while for me to figure it out. But when these lessons struck home, I knew that I had taken my first step toward financial security. I also knew there was big money in buying and selling land.

In the intervening years, I learned many more lessons that I'll pass on to you. But I can truthfully say that none of them has more meaning to me than these principles that I learned at the beginning of my real estate career. And none played a bigger role in my success. Although the journey to financial success may start small, it can result in a big gain.

<u>Think positively. You don't have to start big to get big.</u>

Intelligent Caution + Restraint

Readers Comments

Dear Mr. Stephenson:
 You may cash the money order that I sent you for your book: "A Universal System of Land Transactions." I studied the book and find that not only is it excellently written, but the excellent advice it contains is worth a fortune to anyone. Having your book in my hands is like finding a "pirate treasure chest chuck full of gold doubloons and sparkling jewels." You may be assured that I am very pleased with your book, so my most sincere—THANK YOU!
 Mr. Helmar Burk, Minneapolis, Minnesota

The Reader's Page

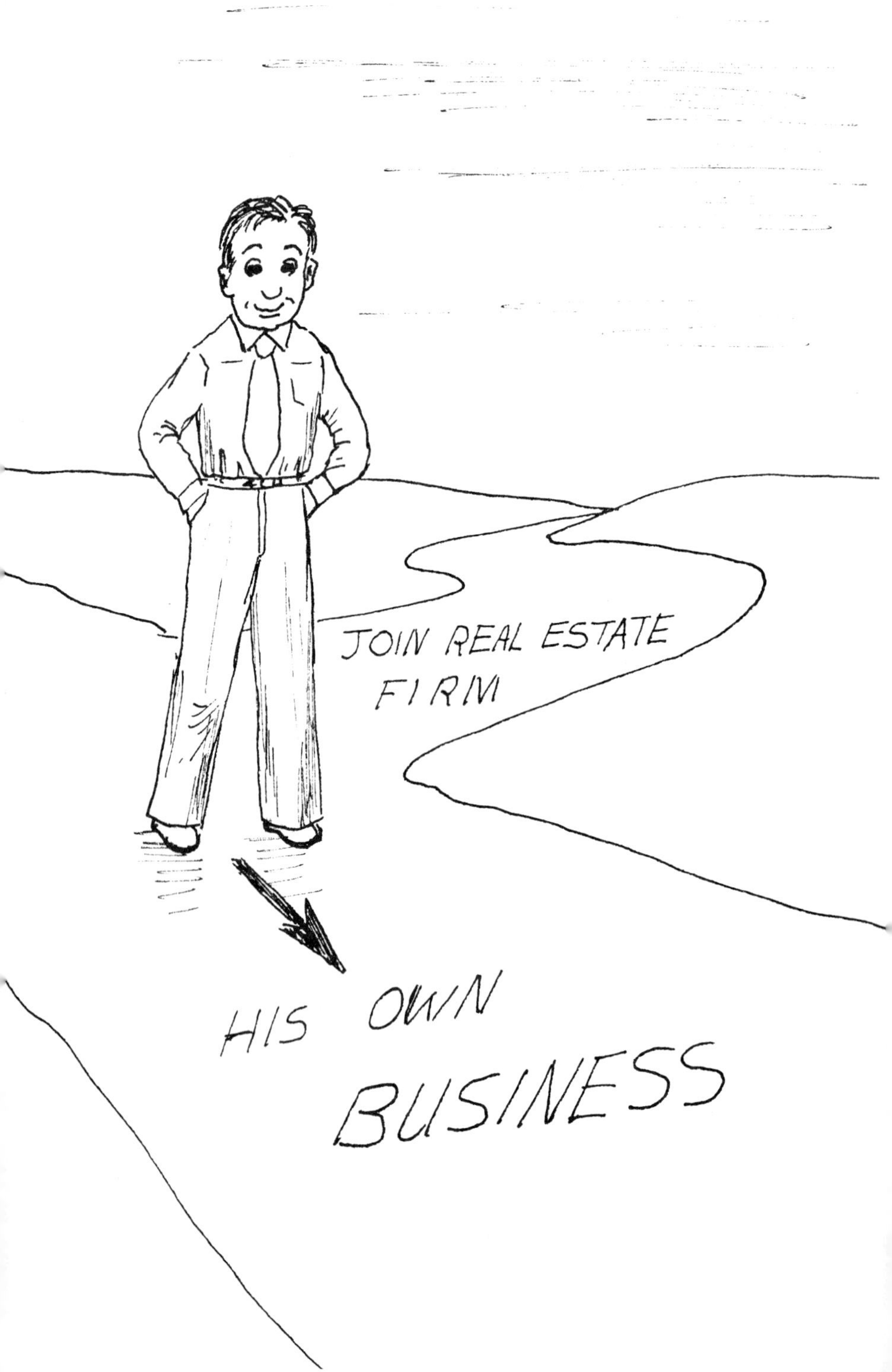
JOIN REAL ESTATE FIRM
HIS OWN BUSINESS

Chapter Five
The Key

Because of my association with my friend's land activity, I gained considerable general knowledge about the land business. Even after I realized the potential it could offer me, I had to make the decision of how to go about actually implementing what I had learned so that I could achieve a measure of financial success.

The idea of starting my own real estate business was one alternative that I naturally considered.

I quickly found out that such a move is a rather extensive process. You must become established in a very competitive market. For example, consider the number of real estate salesmen you know in your home community. How many real estate offices do you regularly pass doing your daily driving? Most people begin their careers by serving an informal apprenticeship under more experienced salesmen and brokers in a community. It is an involved process and often takes years of experience and many sales to achieve any measure of financial security.

Then there is the matter of licensing. Often, college training is necessary. While there may be no formal requirement for such training, it is usually necessary to take courses in order to work within the established framework of real estate laws. Failure to do so can result in having your license revoked.

The more I researched the requirements for starting a real estate business of my own, the more I became convinced that it was not the method under which I could implement the general principles that I had learned from my friend's transaction. The deciding factor was the overhead that I would have to pay if I did move into a real estate office. Office rent, secretarial staff and other operating expenses required more money than I had to spend. In a financial sense, my margin of existence prohibited my thinking in those terms. I therefore ruled out the possibility of establishing or joining a real estate firm.

Yet I still felt that the knowledge I had obtained from observing and participating in my friend's venture was too valuable just to throw aside and forget. I went over the events again and finally found the answer.

My friend had made $60,000 from a land transaction and he didn't have a real estate license. He wasn't an attorney. In fact he didn't even know enough to go to a title company until he asked me for advice. He didn't have the qualifications and he didn't need them because, in a legal sense, they weren't necessary.

This was the key that brought the other lessons together and made me see my avenue to financial success and security.

You don't need a real estate license or any other qualifications to buy and sell land in your own name.

All you need is confidence in your ability and some basic information on how to get started.

The Reader's Page

The Reader's Page

Chapter Six
A Family Approach

After my wife Dianne and I decided that we had acquired enough basic knowledge to become successful in the business of buying and selling land, we had to make an important decision. What should we do to get started? At this point, we still had many unanswered questions. But there was no way to find the answers other than actually going into the venture. We were certain that the venture would work, but we didn't know how long it would be before we began to realize a profit. And we didn't know the amount of profit that we could expect. I was reluctant to quit my job at the beginning in case it took longer than we planned to get our new business off the ground.

We finally found a solution we felt covered all possible angles and provided for any unexpected setbacks. I kept my job selling appliances and Dianne assumed full responsibility for getting the ball rolling on our new road to financial success and security!

You may think that this is somewhat strange. Dianne's background was that of wife and mother. She had very little business background, and she had no special technical knowledge or training that would prepare her to begin a business. Her main function during our marriage had been to take care of the children, the house and me.

But Dianne did have the two things that are necessary to succeed in this venture. She had a great deal of common sense, and she had the desire to become financially successful and secure. She wanted to provide our family with things we needed and things we wanted to make life comfortable. From this point, it was very logical that Dianne should be the one to begin our new business and our new way of life.

She worked hard and it wasn't long before she became a first-class businesswoman. She set up all of our business systems and gathered the information we needed to get started and keep going. She went to the courthouse and made lists of landowners to whom we would mail letters of inquiry asking them if they wanted to sell their land. She established filing systems that enabled us to keep track of whom we had written and what we said to them. As mail came in, she filed it in several categories that let us keep track of the status of various deals that we had been offered. The method she used allowed us to know when and how to follow up on the numerous responses we got from interested landowners. Because we needed to know more about the business we were entering, she contacted people who could help us learn. She talked to public employees, real estate agents, private individuals who knew a lot about land dealing, and other people that we found out about by talking to the obvious sources of information. She bought maps and books that explained land values, how to find certain types of land, tips for the small investor, and the many other things we had to learn and use if we were to become successful in our new business. Because of her research, she was soon able to tell which deals we should follow up immediately, which ones we should let ride for a while, and which landowners we should contact again in the future—sometimes months or even years after our original inquiry. Dianne became the moving force—and the one with "land know-how"—in our business. We were able to conduct our venture in a sensible manner.

During this time, Dianne still had her responsibilities as wife and mother. Often she took the children with her or made arrangements for someone to take care of them if they could not go to her meetings or on her research trips. Her hours were long, and much of her work was done after the children were in bed.

My main function during the first stages of our

[handwritten annotations: GROUND WORK / INITIAL INFORMATION GATHERING / Connections / Know-How / Leg Work / Businesslike / On Luck]

business was to look at the land we considered buying and to decide if it was a good deal. Dianne would locate the land on maps and we would go see it on the weekend. Afterwards, she would take care of follow-up work that was necessary, whether it was doing more research, making an offer, writing more letters, or something else.

Dianne's personal touch and maybe even a little bit of her "woman's intuition" proved to be a bonus to her common sense and desire to learn about the land business. She made suggestions that improved our business systems and became good at finding solutions to problems that others—even those who often had more experience and training in the field—overlooked. One of the most important things she did was to make sure that our deals were well-planned and that they were handled in a businesslike manner.

In the beginning, Dianne devoted a great deal of time to our new business. Sometimes, the tasks were more time-consuming and difficult than necessary. For instance, on our first letters to landowners, she had to write all the letters in longhand because we couldn't afford a typewriter! I'll explain exactly what she did in more detail later. Without Dianne, as you will see, it would have been impossible for us to achieve financial success and security.

By the time I left my job selling appliances, all the groundwork had been laid, the information was gathered, and the business systems were set up. All I had to do was come in and work. Dianne often gave me helpful tips and information that made my job much easier than hers had been.

This type of venture is one that is really a family affair. If your children are old enough, they can help. Financial success and security are a benefit to the entire family. There is no special training or knowledge that you—or anyone—can't learn. What you must have is confidence in yourself and a desire to succeed—and the willingness to work hard.

Readers Comments

Dear Sirs:
   Mr. Gaines and I (Estelle) received your book three days ago and are fascinated with it. We are convinced that your plan will work if approached with level-headedness. So, with this assurance, we would like copies sent to our children, please. Names and addresses are . . .
   Just hope they take advantage of their experience to better their lives and increase their finances. Thanks a million for sharing your knowledge with us.
                              Bill & Estelle Gaines, Palestine, Texas

The Reader's Page

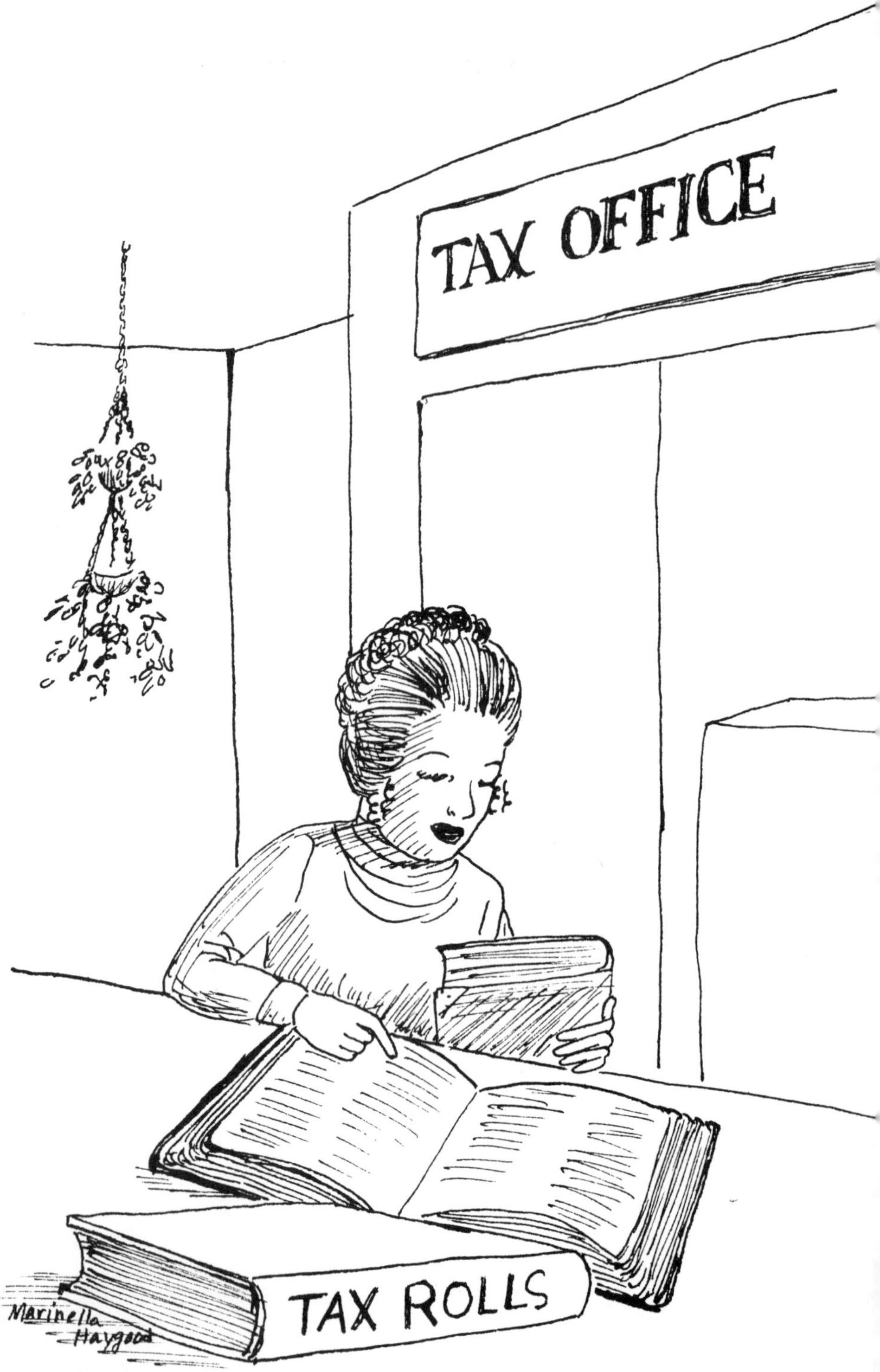
TAX OFFICE
TAX ROLLS
Marinella Haygood

Chapter Seven
Beginning The Venture

If you are like me, you will reject the formal real estate business approach. I am not critizing it. It simply wasn't for me.

Let's expand some of the lessons I cited in a previous chapter.

The first two lessons are closely related and we will consider them together. There are people who want to sell their property and they know how much money they need or want to finalize the transaction. Your job is to identify these people who want to sell their property.

This is one place Dianne became a vital part of our operation. She spent many hours in the county tax office gathering information that we would need for our business.

The county (or parish) tax office has records on every piece of property within that county. These tax records identify the owners of the property, the address and location of the property, the size of the tracts, and the value of the tract that is used for taxing purposes by the county. Each piece of land is identified by an abstract and survey number that usually identifies that tract on the county map.

Your first step is to establish an area of operation for your business. I suggest that you pick a single county and start your operation there. A larger area may be too much to control in the beginning. You don't necessarily have to pick the county where you live. Dianne and I didn't. We picked a rural county that was near our home.

Go to the tax office and ask to see the tax rolls. These are public records and are available for inspection by the public. Because of the obvious value of these records, you will not be allowed to take them from the building. Be sure to take plenty of paper and pencils. You can get a lot of names and addresses in a few hours. The lists you make will become very important in your later business transactions.

What type of land are you looking for? At the beginning, look for tracts of one or more acres. Remember, you are looking for land that an individual can buy or commercial land that is a bargain and below market value. At this stage of your operation, you are interested in buying and selling land as quickly as possible. This is how you will make money.

The tax rolls list the location of the property by abstract and survey number. These numbers usually refer to maps in the county tax office. You can pay to get copies of sections of these maps when needed. The county may also have a county road map that you can purchase for a nominal sum. By taking your road map to the tax office with you, you can mark the general area of land you wish to consider on your own map. If trips to the property become necessary, then you will have an easy guide that tells you how to get there.

I may have mentioned a few terms that confused you. This brings up an important point. *Don't be afraid to ask questions of people who work in the tax office.*

Most public employees are very glad to be of assistance. Treat them with respect and courtesy. Public servants are often underpaid but they continue in their jobs because they have a great desire to help people. Many times they could work in the same type of job in the private sector and make more money. And they know it. Yet they stay in the public job because they want to serve their fellow citizens. Don't rush or push them. If you make a friend of one of the employees in the tax office, he can save you endless hours of searching for information.

For the first go, write down the names of people who live out-of-county or out-of-state. There is a good reason for doing this. If someone in your chosen county decides to sell his land, he will probably call an established real estate firm to handle the land for him. The real estate firms spend long hours competing for local business. To succeed, you should take advantage of a market that has less competition.

But do remember this. Just because a landowner doesn't live in the area where his land is located doesn't mean that he is unfamiliar with the value of his land. Chances are very good that he has a general idea of what the property is worth.

Take yourself as an example. Do you own land outside the area where you live? If so, you have probably paid taxes on it and you are likely to have a reasonable idea of its value.

Several years ago, there was a news story about a Japanese soldier who had been on an island by himself since the end of the war. He had been totally isolated from the rest of humanity for some time. Now this man didn't know the value of land.

But most people are not this removed from what is going on around them. With newspapers, TV, and radio coverage of every event, it is almost impossible to not know something about things happening throughout the world.

Keep this in mind as you undertake the first two lessons in this book. Identify who wants to sell their land and find out how much they need to make the transaction final.

The Reader's Page

The Reader's Page

GET ONTO COUNTY.
↓
go to Co. tax office
↓
Ask for the Tax rolls
↓
get Co. Rd. map
↓
Mark-up Names & Addresses of promising land tracts
/ acre +
↓
Out of State or ~~Town~~ owners
(less competition)

Find sombody to help you understand land values.

Chapter Eight
Get Familiar With Your Home County

By now, you have gone to the tax office and asked to see the tax rolls. You have made friends with an employee of the office who will help you locate specific information you may need, such as finding the property in the map books and transferring it to your county road map.

Before continuing, I would like to emphasize that you don't have to list *all* of the possible tracts of land available in the county before you begin your operation.

Break the tax rolls into arbitrary alphabetical divisions and do one section this month, another section the next month, and so on. Don't expect to determine all of the prospects in one county in one week—or even two. You don't need to and it probably isn't possible. As your wealth increases, the volume of your inquiries can also increase.

But don't rush it. Concentrate on a few at a time.

Now that you have determined the owners of certain property, the number of acres in each tract, and the general land values of your selected area, you are ready to accomplish the second step of finding out who wants to sell his property.

Write a personal letter to each owner telling him that you have become interested in his property and would like to know if he would be interested in selling it.

It should be a straightforward letter with a straightforward request.

Do you want to sell your property and at what price are you willing to sell?

For example, Dianne and I often used letters similar to the one below.

y 23, 1977

ulius T. Lord
e 1
P. U. Box 75
Freeport, New York 11021

Dear Mr. Lord:

We are interested in buying some land in Wharton County. We are interested in the land you own listed in the Parker and Parks Survey, Abstract 50. This survey shows that you have 64.65 acres.

If you are interested in selling, we would like to buy it on terms with a minimum down payment. Since we are individuals, there will be no commission involved. If you need cash, there is a possibility that we can raise it.

We would appreciate hearing from you soon.

Thank you,

Mr. & Mrs. J. E. Stephenson

(Address)

You will receive many replies in which the owner states he isn't interested in selling his land at the present time, but he will keep your request on file for future consideration. File these letters for future use. Dianne and I have bought many pieces of property months or even years after our original inquiry.

By now, you should have a long list of owners, so keep the letters going out at regular intervals.

As the responses come in, there will be many owners who will express an immediate interest in making a deal. We will discuss this later.

But right now, let me give you an important hint.

When Dianne and I got into this business, we literally knew nothing about the value of land in the county in which we began our operation. Because of this, we lost out on some deals from our initial inquiries that we later recognized as superior.

Because of this unfortunate experience on our part, I highly recommend that you become generally familiar with the value of land in your chosen county. Do this before you mail out your first batch of inquiries.

As you go through the tax records and make your lists of landowners, notice the value of the tracts that are used for taxing purposes.

You can also make an appointment with the tax assessor-collector or one of the assistants. These people are knowledgeable and they can give you valuable information about the property values in different areas of the county you have chosen to use as your base.

You don't have to dedicate a month to this task. Just set up appointments with people who have access to information. A little time spent with the right people will add to your store of knowledge. Moreover, the free information they pass on to you will probably save you a lot of money.

As the responses to your inquiries begin to come in, you will be faced with the task of deciding which are good offers and which are not. This is the time when the knowledge you have obtained by reviewing the tax rolls and talking to the right people will serve you well. You will be prepared to make a judgment quickly. Had Dianne and I been able to do this, we would not have lost out on the good bargains in our first stage of operation.

Remember this. You make money on land when you buy it. Not when you sell it. This is fundamental logic.

Why? Because you want to buy land at a price that will allow you to sell again immediately and make a profit.

Don't think for a minute that this type of land is not available. Our transactions will prove otherwise.

The Reader's Page

Notice the value of land tracts from Records, People, Assessors, Transactions, etc.

You EARN when you Buy at a good price that allows you quick sale at a good price.

Getting a loan is not that difficult.

Chapter Nine
Our First Deal

You don't have to start big to get big.
If that principle ever applied to anyone, it certainly applied to the Stephensons.

Remember the advertisement that stated our total income in 1967 was about $12,000 with debts of approximately half that much.

With four children to support, this is probably the smallest financial base with which we could have started. And yet we did make a success of our business.

We were somewhat unsure of ourselves in the beginning, so I did not quit my job immediately.

Dianne went to the County Clerk's office to perform those tasks previously described. When she had developed a list of landowners that we considered sufficient, we began writing our letters of inquiry.

The response came almost immediately. In fact, we received so many responses that we didn't know how to handle all of them.

This initial failure to act quickly cost us some sales. As I explained, this is why it is important for you to have some idea of the general value of the land in your selected county.

Despite our confusion, within a short time we had identified a good piece of land being offered at a low price by a willing seller.

This particular reply was from a trust company out-of-state. The trust handled the estate of 110 acres of land that was the subject of our inquiry. They wrote that the land was for sale at the price of $325 per acre.

As inexperienced as we were, we realized that this was a potentially good offer.

After two days of looking for the land—I told you we were green—we finally located it.

We did some further research and determined that it was the type of land that we could sell immediately and make a good profit, if worse came to worse.

We were ready to move, right? Not quite. We were broke.

Even though we were broke, we did have a piece of paper from a trust company which said it would sell us 110 acres of land for $325 per acre cash. I took this letter to an official of a Houston bank where I already had an account.

After giving some background information and on the basis of that letter, my banker agreed to loan me $500 on a three-month signature note.

So this was how we got started.

Remember the fourth lesson? *Use a title company* and get professional help.

This was my next step.

I wrote the officer of the trust company handling the land that we accepted the offer of $325 per acre. I enclosed a cashier's check for $500 to be used as earnest money and I asked him to prepare the contract.

About one week later, we received a copy of the contract with instructions to go to a Houston title company selected by the trust and to sign it. By signing the contract, I was agreeing to pay for the land at the time of closing.

From the representative of the title company, I learned that it takes about four to six weeks for all of the necessary investigative work to be done on establishing clear ownership of a piece of property.

I signed the earnest money contract on a Wednesday afternoon.

You will recall that the fifth lesson is to *know how to sell land.*

This was my next step.

I ran a classified ad in the Friday paper of one of Houston's major metropolitan newspapers. The advertisement was simple and to the point. It included the basic information a potential buyer would want.

> BARGAIN! BARGAIN! BARGAIN!
> Four miles from. . . . This land
> has good road frontage . . .
> Surrounding land sells for $700-$800
> per acre. Individual is selling for cash
> and asking $525 per acre.

I believe that this ad demonstrates how to sell land effectively.

Look at the selling price of my land and compare it to the market value of surrounding land. It is well below other comparable tracts.

That is a guiding principle of my business. Buy land at a price you know that you can sell again immediately and make a profit.

Once the advertisement appeared, the phone didn't stop ringing. I made several appointments to show the land to prospective buyers. I kept in contact with Dianne by telephone and she would tell prospects where to meet me on the outskirts of town.

On one such call, Dianne told me to come home. There was a man waiting to see me who wanted to pay cash for the land. She had talked to him earlier in the day while I was showing the land to some other prospective buyers. In the meantime, he had asked the location and had gone to see it for himself. It was choice property and he decided he wanted to buy it so he had come back to the house to talk about terms of the contract.

We talked and agreed to the terms. He selected the title company. That title company prepared his earnest money contract in which he agreed to buy the land from me once I produced a clear title. He accepted my condition of putting $10,000 earnest money down on the contract.

I told the "closer" (my buyer's title company) that I would bring all of the necessary paperwork to our appointment the following Monday. I showed the attorney in charge a copy of my contract with the first owner and explained that the trust handling the land wanted to use another title company for their transaction with me.

The attorney stated that cooperation between title companies in such matters is routine procedure and he agreed to handle the situation. This transaction is known as "double closing."

The net result: Dianne and I grossed $20,500 profit from our very first transaction. And we had accomplished it by borrowing $500 to pay for an earnest money contract.

In our wildest dreams, we had never envisioned making $20,500 at one time.

I went to the bank; paid off our bank loans; paid our house payments one year in advance; and quit my job. I wanted to devote my full time to this new and promising career in real estate.

I woke up nights wondering if I was still dreaming!

The Reader's Page

NO BLOOD NEEDED ON THIS CASE, DOCTOR.
EARNEST MONEY CONTRACT
Chart
Marinella Haygood
EARNEST MONEY IS NOT BLOOD MONEY.

Chapter Ten
Nagging Questions

I have described how Dianne and I used our system on our first land deal. But you probably still have some nagging questions. Therefore, I will give you a brief summary that may help to clear up some of these questions and more fully explain our system.

I had signed an earnest money contract agreeing to pay the trust in charge of the land $35,750 in cash for the land within a specific period of time. You may be asking how a person who has to borrow his first $500 for the earnest money contract can be stupid enough to commit himself to paying $35,750.

The answer to your question is simple. Only buy land that you know you can sell for a profit. When you sell land, don't be so greedy that you expect to become wealthy off that one deal. I have followed this principle strictly and have never been burned in a deal. This is especially important in the beginning of your operations.

Since that first transaction, I have learned other implications and advantages in using this strategy. Many investment groups and corporations often buy property by negotiating very favorable terms. For example, they agree to pay interest for only five years with no payment of interest on the principle of the note. In plain language, this simply means that they are speculating in the purchasing of land.

They are buying the land on the basis of what the future market may hold in store. Often, they will agree to pay astronomical sums of money for property, but they will demand terms which require only a minimum payment for several years. This enables them to make these small minimum payments regularly while they hold the land and wait for the market to develop.

If the market doesn't develop, they simply stop making payments and the land goes back to the original owner. Actually they are making regular payments for the speculative use of the land.

This is the standard method of making money in the real estate business. Find some land; use a minimum amount of money to buy it; and wait for the market to develop before selling.

Investment groups, corporations, and very wealthy individuals can afford to do this on the big level. You are doing it on a small level. But it is a level which is just as effective because you only buy land for which there is already a market.

When I signed that earnest money contract, my total risk was $500—not $35,750.

The earnest money contract states your intentions to buy the land. This is the extent of your agreement with the seller. The contract is not a contract "in blood."

Analyze our first transaction again, and I think you will agree that we followed the rules of our universal system. Throughout the years, I have never strayed from the basic lessons that make the system work. As a result, I have never entered a deal in which I have not made a financial gain.

There is much you can do on your own, but there will be many times that you need professional help. Don't ever be afraid to seek the professional help of people who know more about certain things than you.

Good advice is profitable advice. Seek it at every opportunity.

The Reader's Page

Only land
Buy or ppty.
for which there
already exists a market-

↓

At a minimal am't
of money
↓
then sell it
wisely

Always seek
professional
(profitable) advice.
Early & @ every
opportunity

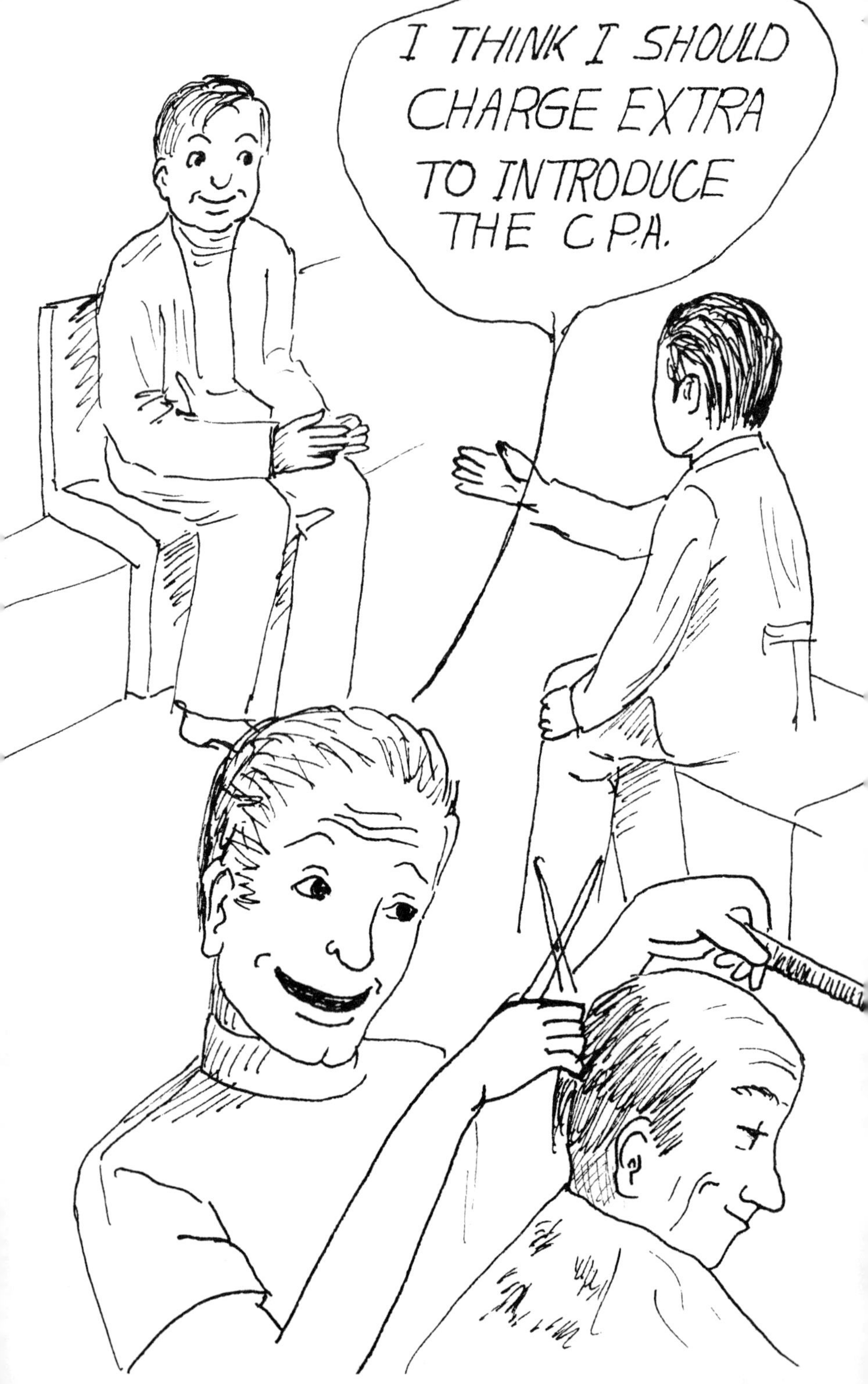
I THINK I SHOULD CHARGE EXTRA TO INTRODUCE THE C.P.A.

Chapter Eleven
Meet My CPA

Business partners often meet in the most unlikely places.

You may recall from the Prologue that Dr. Shaw mentioned he met me when I took my dog to his clinic for treatment. I have forgotten the fee he charged me for that service, but I do know it ended by his making quite a bit of money beyond the actual fee. As a result of our meeting, I was able to guide him in investments that proved quite profitable for the investment group with which he was associated.

While my first deals had certainly been successful, I will admit that my CPA has helped me manage my business profits very effectively. Neal Elden, my personal CPA, has given me good advice on all of my land transactions from the time we entered a business agreement.

A good CPA will take your efforts and newfound knowledge of land and guide you through the intricacies of tax laws and other necessary technicalities.

I first met Neal in the barbershop. He was explaining to the barber how people used equity in the land business to obtain a geometric-type progression of their wealth.

When I heard "land business," my ears perked up. I paid attention to the rest of his conversation with his barber. It didn't take long for me to realize that this was the exact man with whom I needed to talk.

After some initial discussions, he rearranged my financial statement to more accurately reflect my true net worth.

Because of his work, it was then much easier for me to obtain financing from lending institutions. This was essential in order for me to branch out into more lucrative land deals.

I explained my idea of not wanting to hold land for a long period of time, and I told him of my desire to use a quick turnover approach in my business. He told me that this was very sound and logical thinking.

The secret, if indeed there is such a thing, to making money by using my system is to have a very clear definition of your goals. Start small. Get a little bigger. And then get a little bigger. At some point, you will be ready to make the *really big* deal. Generally, the big one has to be preceded by several small ones.

In business terms, this is consolidation of equity or the accumulation of greater wealth.

If you start small, say the $20,000 I made in our first deal, and through a series of transactions begin to add to that equity, it is easy to see that it doesn't take long before you are talking about big money. For this reason, when you start be willing to begin with less profit than you think you might achieve on any one particular deal.

Remember. It won't be long until you are getting numerous responses from your regular letter campaigns. There will be a number of landowners who respond and they will keep you busy for quite some time.

Use a certain percentage of the profits from your first deal to improve your business system. Dianne and I found this to be a good plan.

For instance, you will probably want to invest in a good file cabinet and ownership maps. You can then easily keep track of owners you have written. As the responses come in, you may find it useful to file the responses in these categories: offers to be considered, owners to write in the future (there will be many who are undecided when they receive your letter), owners who give an immediate "no" to your inquiry, and miscellaneous. Remember that many people who say they are not interested in selling their land at the present time may be the very ones who contact you at a later date wanting to sell their land. Or if you write them again, they may decide to sell although they might not have actually been planning to sell. Financial conditions change very quickly and the people who own land are no exception. So be sure to save these letters and put them in a file that you know means to contact them at a later date.

Any investment you make toward improving the professional organization of your business is a sound investment.

Also remember that you will need to set aside an amount to pay the professionals whom you will need to consult from time to time. Some of these will include a CPA, an attorney, a title company, and others knowledgeable in the land business.

One point you must keep in mind is that it will not take many small deals before you reach the time when you can go after that big one. You must prepare yourself to be ready to recognize it and take the proper action when the time comes. It is also important to remember that you may not have a long time to act. By organizing your business affairs from the beginning of your new career, you will be ready to move quickly when that big deal does come along.

At this time, I would call the $20,000 profit we made on our first land transaction a small deal. But at the time we made it, it was the biggest amount of money we had ever made.

It all depends on your perspective. Like Dianne and me, you will change your financial thinking too. Your point of view will become big.

Just think positively.

The Reader's Page

The Reader's Page

Hold on to land or property briefly
↓
quick turnover
↓
Consolidate equity
↓
Accumulation of
Greater wealth

Get in sombody's way and you can sell your land.

Chapter Twelve
More Deals, More Profits

Frankly, by now I hope that you have developed some confidence in me. I have given you the background on why I call my method of buying and selling land a universal system. I have given you specific information on my first deal and some additional advice I have learned from my CPA. I have stressed the need to depend upon professional people at the start for the type of expert assistance which can save you great expense later.

You should now have a broad understanding of what the system is all about. And you should be able to follow the reasoning behind some of the other transactions I'm going to describe.

The second deal we made was one of the most complicated transactions I have ever had to complete. I'm including this description because it reveals that it won't take long for you to begin recognizing good buys.

Three weeks after Dianne and I had closed out our first deal for the $20,000 profit, we received another inquiry.

In their reply to our regular letter inquiry, the owners stated that they had already sold the land I was asking about, but they said they owned an undivided interest in a 177-acre tract of land. They asked if I would be interested in that property.

Dianne and I went to the courthouse in the county where the land was located and looked it up. The land that the owners were offering consisted of undivided interest in 53 acres of land. The total tract was only 500 feet wide and over a mile long. But adjoining land was scheduled for use as a subdivision. It was selling in wooded lots at about $3,000 per acre. Since the land under consideration was wooded as well I felt that if we could buy out the other owners we would have some excellent property and be able to realize substantial profit from this investment.

That evening when we came home, Dianne wrote the owners of the 53 acres and said that we would accept their offer of $50.00 per acre cash.

The next day, Dianne went back to the same county courthouse and in the tax room she made a list of the names and addresses of all the other owners of the 177 acres.

That night we repeated the process. This time we began the letters by writing that Mr. & Mrs. So & So were selling their undivided interest for $50 per acre and that we were making them and all the other owners an offer to buy their undivided interest at $50 per acre.

The owners of this 177-acre tract had owned it for years. It had been unprofitable property for two reasons. First, the property was isolated; and second, the undivided interest made it impossible for the owners to do anything with their land unless all the other owners agreed to suggestions made by any one owner. Within a short time, they all wrote back. Every owner accepted our offer of $50 per acre. Because of the problems involved in owning undivided land, they felt it was to their benefit to realize an immediate profit out of the land rather than continuing in a joint ownership that was not profitable.

Naturally we accepted all the offers to sell at $50 per acre. Then we took our earnest money contract to the owners of the adjoining subdivision. I asked $500 per acre for our contract. One investor in the subdivision stated he would submit our offer to the other investors. Ten days later he gave me a written offer of $325 per acre. Dianne and I accepted the offer as it was for cash and we would profit in the amount of $48,000.

Again, we had learned of a very good bargain simply because of our letters going out at regular intervals.

As you become more involved in your land business, you will probably notice that many people own undivided interest in land. These people will be excellent prospects to contact simply because holding undivided interest in land is usually unprofitable. People can't do anything with the land and if they are making any kind of profit at all, it is usually very small. The problems of dealing with joint owners are often complicated. For this reason, people who own an undivided interest are often willing to sell—and at a reasonable or even bargain price. There are hundreds—even thousands—of owners who are in this situation and often they will jump at the opportunity to sell what they consider to be property that is more trouble than it's worth. It is true that contacting all owners of any tract can be a time-consuming process; but also remember that it's often well worth your time and efforts.

In the strictest sense, this inquiry had been a failure. We didn't purchase or sell the land in which we were originally interested.

But from another standpoint, it was very successful. It brought us a firm offer to sell another piece of land.

This dramatically illustrates the first two points of my universal system.

(1) *There are people who want to sell their property right now and they know how much money they need to finalize the transaction.*

(2) *Identify who wants to sell their property.*

One trip to the courthouse in which we had implemented these two principles grossed Dianne and me over $60,000 in profits—on our first two transactions!

The system works.

Readers Comments

Dear Mr. & Mrs. Stephenson:
 Having read through your book, I am amazed at your success in the business of buying and selling land. I am so impressed by your guts and "down to earth" personality that I have enclosed the fee for one year's subscription to your newsletter.
 I have thought about buying land for investment purposes, but could never figure out how to raise the required capital. At one time I was considering buying land at sheriff sales, but I soon learned that land bought this way cannot be sold or improved upon until after holding the land 18 months . . . . Here's hoping that we hit it off good together in 1977!

Mr. Stanley M. Woodring, Morgantown, New York

The Reader's Page

Contact owners of undivided interest ↑ Prime Prospects

AVOID THE BIDDING WAR!

Chapter Thirteen
Accumulate Your Wealth

Even though our first two deals grossed us approximately $68,000—before taxes, of course—Dianne and I never turned our backs on a good land deal just because it involved less money. We remembered the sound advice of maintaining our effort toward the accumulation of wealth. It is the accumulation that will eventually allow you to make the really big deal.

With this point in mind, we entered our third transaction with another trust company.

They had received our inquiry concerning 80 acres of land in our home-base county and wrote us that they would sell the land for $325 per acre. We immediately accepted and sent them an earnest money contract for $500 with instructions to have a title company prepare the agreement.

This deal went much like the first, but it was smaller in proportion.

We didn't mind, though, because the $7,700 profit was still big news to us.

The transaction involved the same double-closing procedures employed in the first transaction.

Our fourth sale was again a direct result of our blanket letter inquiries to landowners in a selected county.

A lady called from a pay phone and said that she and her husband had decided to sell some land they owned and she would be interested in working out an agreement with us for cash. Since she had no phone, I told her to write me a letter and state her best price and be sure to include the adress so that we could get back in touch with her. She said that she would discuss it with her husband.

Two days later, we got her letter. She and her husband had decided that they would take $250 an acre for the land. Even before looking at the land, Dianne and I felt that this was a good bargain. We went to see the land that afternoon.

When we actually saw the land, we knew that we wanted to buy it. The land had an excellent square shape with good road frontage. I felt that it was probably worth about $700 or $750 an acre.

Since there was no way to contact her by telephone, Dianne and I drove to her house and accepted her $250 per acre for the property. I said that if she knew an attorney in her part of town, we would take her deed and the proper papers to get an earnest money contract drawn that afternoon. We set the closing for 90 days. After the title was ready, I took the earnest money contract with a $1,000 check made to the title company and I was then in a position to make improvements on the land I planned to sell.

Before I sell a tract of land, I always make sure that it is in a condition to make a favorable impression on a prospective buyer. I figure that for every $100 I spend in making improvements on the property I raise the selling price about $1,000. I have found this practice to be very profitable.

The next day, I took my truck with a tractor and shredder and the next few days were spent mowing the land. I painted the gate and had two loads of gravel put in a large culvert that was on the property. When I finished, it was a very neat piece of property.

Two weeks later, I put an ad in the paper and sold it for cash at $525 an acre.

My buyer put up his earnest money at a different title company. There was a 90-day waiting period before we could close it out. But when closing came, we made approximately $13,500.

Avoid the bidding war!

One of the soundest pieces of advice I can give is never haggle with prospective buyers over the price of land. The situation can develop easily, and you need to be prepared to react in a way that will not cost you money. Always be prepared to make a firm offer when one is requested, but don't ever get into a bidding war. You must expect to make some mistakes when you begin, but try to avoid this one.

We were inexperienced when we made the mistake of talking too soon. This eventually cost us an extra $50 per acre on 53-1/2 acres of land.

We received a reply to one of our letters from a man who said he was willing to sell his land at $325 per acre. Dianne and I went to the property and asked a neighbor the value of the land. The neighbor knew exactly where the land was located. In fact he had been trying to buy that very property for several years!

Immediately, he asked us if the owner wanted to sell his land. Even though we were inexperienced, we realized that we had "tipped our hand."

That afternoon we wrote the owner that we accepted his offer of $325 per acre. But the interested neighbor was also acting quickly. He called the owner and after talking to him, he offered $350 per acre, outbidding our offer by $25 per acre.

We made the mistake that was to be so costly when we wrote back and made a new offer of $360 per acre to top the neighbor's offer.

The owner called to tell us the neighbor had now offered $375 per acre. But he also said that he was willing to accept an offer of $380 per acre from us.

How did we handle this situation?

In the only way possible. We contacted our attorney.

The lawyer wrote the owner a letter stating that he had originally offered the land for sale at $325 an acre and that we had accepted this offer in writing. He told the owner that we would make a counteroffer of $375 per acre, the amount that the neighbor had finally offered. If our offer was not accepted, we would sue.

Although our inexperience had cost us $50 more per acre than we had intended to pay, we still made a good deal. Our profit was some $35,000 when we sold the land.

The fact that we had used the services of an attorney to stop the bidding war is important.

Did we take advantage of the owner? Not at all. He got just $5 less per acre than what he wanted to sell. All we had made him do was honor his agreement to sell the land to us.

We learned quickly that there are times when you have to represent your interests forcefully and intelligently.

I don't blame the owner for getting two people involved in a bidding war. He wanted to make as much money on his land as he could.

Remember our advice to become generally familiar with land values in your selected county and you can avoid this problem.

The Reader's Page

Don't get involved in Bidding.
↓
(Different than Bargaining)

The Reader's Page

Chapter Fourteen
The Big Deal Will Come

I have mentioned that I consider myself to be a rather sophisticated land dealer. I think that the description of our next deal will give you an idea of the great amount of knowledge that can be obtained in a relatively short period of time. This is an interesting example of the *Big Deals* that come as a result of the constant, ever-increasing accumulation of wealth.

This particular big deal enabled us to become very selective in our pursuit of land transactions. It also enabled Dianne and me to go into semiretirement and work toward improving our ranch.

Again, don't expect to make a deal like this in your first week of using our system, but do expect it to come eventually.

In 1972, Dianne and I started working our home-base county for the second time. We went through the tax records again, making new lists of property owners. Afterwards we went through our files to determine which of the owners we had already contacted on our first letter-writing effort. (This is one reason why it is important to keep files on every letter you write, the response you receive, etc.) The last time we had worked this county was some three and a half years earlier. We had made some great buys then, including our ranch, and we hoped to make some good ones on our second letter campaign in the county.

By this time, we had found out that a second letter-mailing effort could be just as productive as the first mailing. People are constantly selling, buying, inheriting, and acquiring land. Others decide that they want to sell land they have owned for years for the numerous reasons we mentioned earlier. Don't ever think that just because you have worked an area in the past that it shouldn't be worked again in the future. In fact, the second time can be even more profitable than the first. On this second try with our home-base county, we grossed over a half million dollars in ten months' time!

In March of 1972, we received a telephone call from a Houston real estate agent. He told us his client, who was out-of-state, had received a letter from us saying that we wanted to buy his 395 acres. He hadn't thought about selling it, but had decided, as a direct result of our letter, that he would rather realize a profit from the land than continue to hold it. The real estate agent was authorized to offer us the land at $1,500 per acre. The agent and I set up an appointment for that afternoon at the property location.

The land proved to be excellent. It was a wooded piece of property on the high side of a river and it had a lot of good road frontage. I knew that it would make a beautiful tract for subdividing purposes.

The agent said that the owner had inherited the land some years ago from his father. As far as he knew, the land had never been surveyed. (When it was surveyed, it proved to have more acreage than we thought.) The owner's family had owned it since the Texas land grants, and the property was fenced.

As it turned out, the owner very seldom went to the land. He leased it and had decided to sell it since he never used it himself. The agent also said that if I didn't want it he would put a group of investors together and buy it himself.

We drove over the acreage in my truck and it looked just as good from one side of the property as it did from the other. I told him I would buy it.

We arranged for my attorney and his attorney to draw up the earnest money contract for $5,000 so that I could begin purchasing the land. The terms of purchase were $1,500 per acre with $80,000 down and interest to be paid for only the first five years of a 15-year contract.

The real estate agent was happy. The owner was paying a 5% commission to sell the land. The $35,378 commission he was making involved very little effort on his part.

Then I began the process of searching for a buyer to whom I could sell the land. I ran an ad in both of Houston's major newspapers for faster results.

A group responded to my inquiries and agreed to pay me $2,100 per acre for the land. I tentatively agreed to the offer they made, but I told them that they would have to meet certain conditions. They knew the value of the land and so they were more than willing to work with me.

I informed them that I wanted to have a capital gain on this transaction since we were talking about approximately $300,000 in potential profit. The group was willing to work with me in solving my special tax problem because they knew they could sell the land for $3,000 per acre. I was only asking $2,100 per acre.

My tax problem was tricky. It kept my CPA, my attorney and the attorneys representing the group busy trying to find a way that would allow me to obtain an immediate capital gain.

The final solution was found by Dianne!

The group paid $130,000 down at the time of my closing of the property at $1,500 per acre, but the property remained in my name. From this $130,000, I took $80,000 and paid off the required down payment of my contract to buy the land from the original owner.

I then met all the terms of my contract with the original seller. The prospective new owners—the group—had paid me $130,000 down to insure that I could achieve this requirement.

At the time of the closing, I gave my buyers the option to pay the agreed price of $2,100 an acre for the land within six months. Six months later, they exercised their option and I received another $10,000 in cash plus a second lien note of $280,000.

With an initial investment of $5,000, I was able to use $130,000 of someone else's money to achieve the closing on a land deal which I wouldn't have believed possible several years earlier.

There are several points that you should learn from this particular deal.

The first is to buy *only* land that you know you can sell again and make at least a minimal profit.

Be willing to sell the land at a price that will enable the next owner to sell and make a profit too. If I had tried to make all the money that was possible from this particular land, the group that bought the land would not have been willing to work with me on my special tax problem. But they knew that they could sell the land for $900 more per acre than I was asking. Everyone involved in this deal made a profit. This is the key to successful buying and selling of land.

If you remember this philosophy and enter transactions with it in mind, you will certainly succeed.

The Reader's Page

Marinella Haygood

Chapter Fifteen
More Sophisticated Transactions

As you become more sophisticated, you will learn the many ways in which land can be used. This knowledge will be your avenue to more complicated land transactions.

One evening in 1968 we received a call from a Dallas woman who owned an undivided interest in some land. She and the other heirs had agreed to sell. She told us that she and the five other heirs owned about 1,276 acres of grasslands. About 1,000 acres were used as grazing and ranching land and the remaining 276 acres were used for rice farming.

She talked about half an hour explaining why she and the other heirs had agreed to sell the land. They had an undivided interest in the land they wanted to sell to get their affairs in shape. She said that having an undivided interest, even with close friends, was a real problem. If some of the heirs passed away, then there were more heirs to deal with and more new problems. These particular people were all well-off financially and most were professional doctors and dentists. Money was not a problem to them; they simply wanted to get rid of something they considered bothersome. She named the price of $400 an acre as their selling price.

Dianne and I drove out the next day and looked at the land. As it turned out, $400 was a very good price. But we wanted to buy it in separate tracts and separate notes. It had about five miles of road frontage and we wanted to subdivide it.

I called her back that evening and we agreed to the terms that she had stated the previous evening. We agreed to meet at a Houston title company in two days.

This was actually a formality as she brought the other heirs with her to sign the necessary papers. I put up $1,000 in an earnest money contract and the closing was scheduled for 120 days.

I put one stipulation into the contract. I agreed to pay $50,000 down, but I obtained 10-year financing on five different notes, representing my wishes to divide the land into five tracts.

Why did I want to divide the land? Because I felt that the large acreage involved was too expensive for most people to afford. The land had ample road frontage and I decided that it would be very easy to sell it in separate tracts. This was the purpose for having the earnest money contract reflect a five-note agreement on five different tracts of varying sizes.

The following day I put a classified advertisement in both of Houston's major metropolitan newspapers. I wanted the widest possible exposure on this deal.

Within 15 days, I had arranged to sell the first 420 acres at $475 per acre for $76,000 down. My buyer agreed to assume the notes for tracts A and B. Eventually there was a double closing on this tract.

I was now in a position to pay off the entire $50,000 down payment to which I was committed and obtain title to the remainder of the land. Within three months, I had sold the balance of the acreage as divided and grossed some $98,000.

There is an interesting side note to this story. Two days after we signed the earnest money contract, a real estate broker drove up to our home one Sunday afternoon. He told me that he and his family had been leasing the acreage for years and he had asked to buy the land several times. He was astonished that we had been able to buy land that he had asked about several times. He personally knew the owners and had told them that if they ever decided to sell, he wanted the first opportunity to buy.

The only reply I had was to tell him about our letter system. It looked to me as if the owners of the 1,276 acres were not ready to sell until they received our letter and they had circulated it among themselves. They just decided to sell and had named the lady that called as their spokesman.

If we had not written them, in my opinion they would have eventually listed it with a real estate agent and we would never have had the opportunity to buy when we did at the price we settled for. It may be that a written desire worked better with these particular owners than an informal conversation. Perhaps the owners hadn't really taken the leaseholder's request as something to be considered seriously. Maybe they like the business approach of a letter. For whatever reason, our letter campaign had worked again. We had been able to buy land that others wanted. But we were the ones who succeeded in getting the opportunity to buy.

Variations of the basic principles can be utilized to effectively buy and sell land that may not look like a good deal on your first glance. These different methods of handling land will come to you easily after you have been involved in your business for a short time.

The Reader's Page

The Reader's Page

Variations
↓
Subdivide
↓
to Tracts
↓
easier to sell
↓
5 Different notes when u Buy

↓
this was
Joint ppty

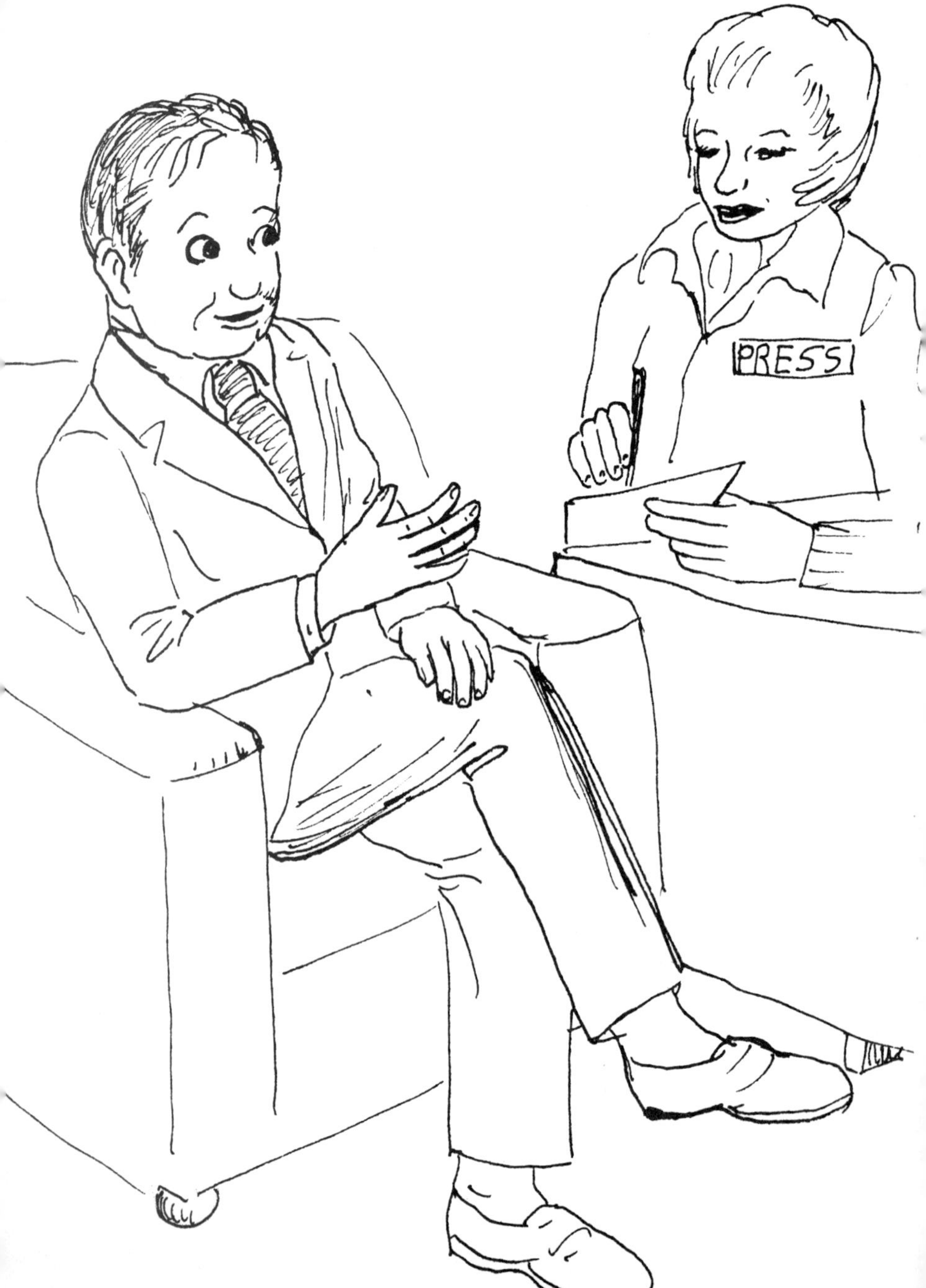
PRESS

Chapter Sixteen
We Make The Headlines

Dianne and I started our land venture in 1967 with no experience and very little knowledge of the actual business intricacies of buying and selling property.

We both think that one of the highlights of our lives was when a *Houston Post* reporter, Adine Lundgren, came to our home to interview us.

The *Houston Post* is one of the more respected newspapers in the nation with a circulation of approximately 500,000. When the reporter's story appeared on the front page of the BUSINESS section we were very proud.

I decided to reprint that story in this book because it explains a great deal about my philosophy of buying and selling land. It should serve as encouragement to you. Once you get into this business, you too will become a person whose views on buying and selling land will be sought.

Land Firm Serves
Small Buyers

By Adine Lundgren

Copyright 1972: *The Houston Post*
Reprinted by Permission

Jim Stephenson has parlayed an understanding of people—people who are suspicious of city slickers and real estate specialists—into a small fortune.

"Some people don't like to buy from real estate people just as some people don't like to buy a car from a lot although they will buy a car from an individual," says

Stephenson, who lives in Richmond 30 miles southwest of Houston.

Additionally, "land may have a sentimental value for people who would rather sell their land to someone who is going to use it for himself rather than subdivide it or use the acreage for a garbage dump," he continues.

He discovered that a blanket mailing of letters with a personal touch to landowners could unearth good buys.

"We had a hard struggle. We knew nothing about buying and selling land at first," the 42-year old Stephenson recalls.

The $130,000 Stephenson says he grossed last year indicates he learned some.

He concedes, of course, that there's an art to buying and selling.

"I've been buying and selling something all my life," he added.

Stephenson specialized in land a small investor can afford.

"You have so many people whose whole ambition is to buy 100 acres of land.

"So most of the land I look for is in the working man's category—$300 - $700 an acre.

"If you get over $800 an acre, a man looking for a tract of land that he can pay for and retire on can't afford it," Stephenson said. . . .

Thereafter, Stephenson and his wife Dianne, went to the county courthouse to make a list of persons who owned 10 acres or more of land. A letter to each followed.

"Dianne writes a real good personal letter," he said.

His wife adds, "These people get stacks of letters from real estate people."

Timing is important, she points out. After receiving a letter asking Stephenson to make an offer, "I'll let it go stale. If I get over-anxious and nervous, they get over-anxious or nervous," Mrs. Stephenson says.

Out of 40 letters, five will say, "Make me an offer," Stephenson says.

"We couldn't afford maps at first," Mrs. Stephenson remembers. "We spent all of our time driving. We couldn't have found a piece of land if someone had given it to us." Since buying his first land, Stephenson has bought tracts in Fort Bend and Brazoria Counties. He isn't active, however, toward Conroe.

Of the latter area he says, "That's developers' land, which sells for around $2,000 an acre. If you buy that land, you have to sell it to a group of investors."

Commercial property doesn't appeal either, "because it takes too much money and it takes too long to find people to buy it."

Essentially, "I specialize in making a better than normal buy and selling the land at a good price."

"You have to buy property reasonable enough so that you can sell it reasonable enough and still make a profit.

"I sell 95 percent of my property below the appraised cost. I know how much money I've got in a piece of land and I'll take a fast turnover by selling below market value to get on to something else," Stephenson explains.

A novice land buyer "can get hung up so bad on land. You can get land on a dead end road or with a garbage dump close by.

"Don't buy land without an easement or a road to it so you won't be landlocked. And you want at least one-fourth of the mineral rights," Stephenson advises.

With his tractor, Stephenson cuts high weeds and cleans up his land before he sells it, "so it looks neat."

As to where to buy land, he recalls, "Someone told us the best way to buy land is to buy land that's in somebody's way. For example, a freeway, a shopping center, road or subdivision.

In selling land, "I don't list property with real estate companies because they are going to get tied up and not do anything with it. But if real estate people bring out a buyer, then I'll pay a commission," Stephenson says.

Generally, "real estate people can get more money for

land than you or I," he continues. Yet the thought of paying a commission deters many persons from dealing with real estate firms, Stephenson adds.

"I'm not the smartest man you ever knew. But as long as I can make a good buy and sell at a good price, I guess I can pay my bills," Stephenson concludes.

Readers Comments

Dear Mr. & Mrs. Stephenson,
Just a note to tell you I think your book is about to open a great new future for me! I wish you had written it twenty years ago.
I will send you the $92.50 for the newsletter and will have a lot of questions and will be very thankful for your direction.
This opportunity comes to me at a time in my life when I am no longer able to report for work at 7:45 a.m. and work an eight-hour day, so it is of great importance to me to do all you have outlined correctly.
Mrs. A. Hill, San Antonio, Texas

The Reader's Page

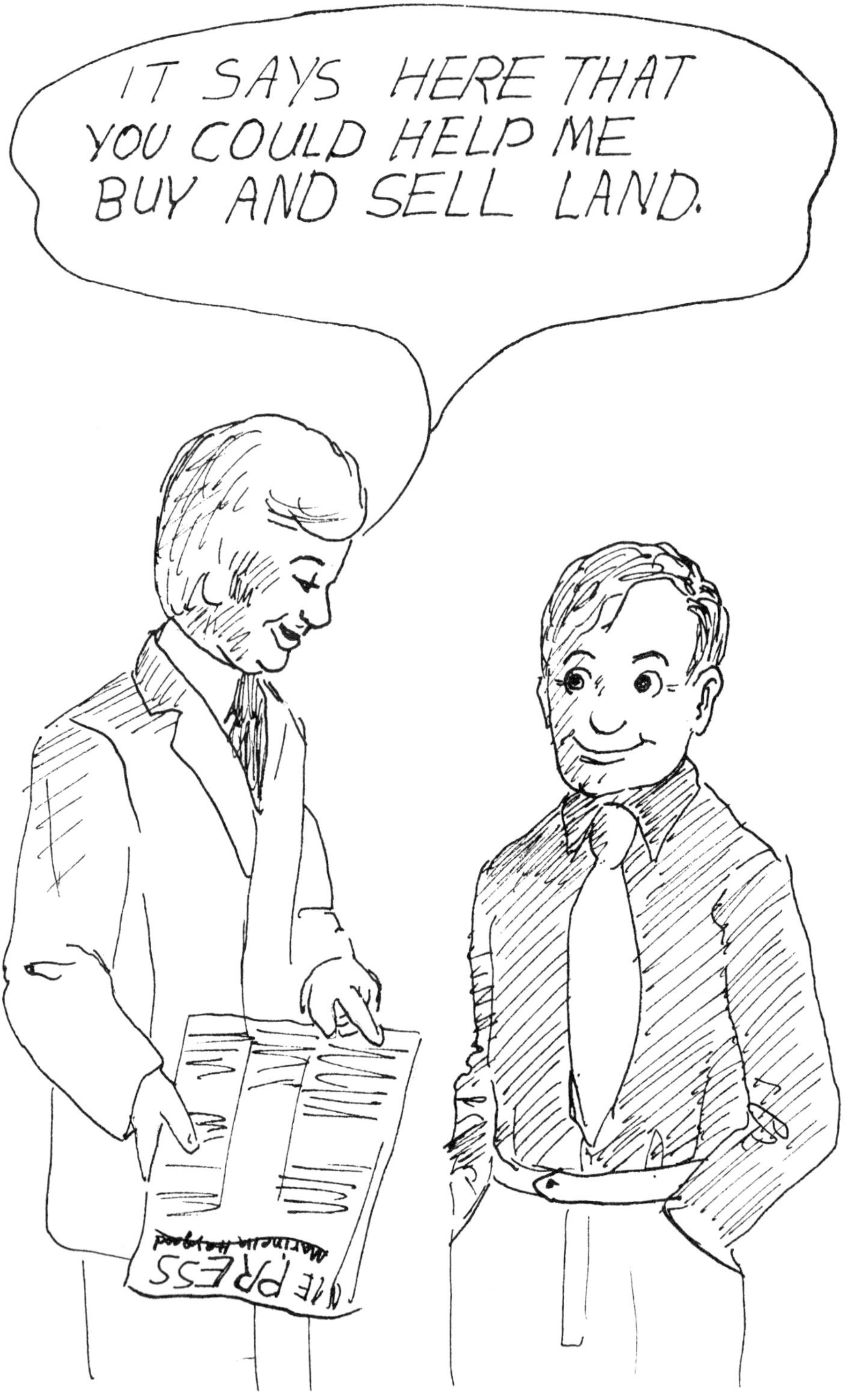
IT SAYS HERE THAT YOU COULD HELP ME BUY AND SELL LAND.

Chapter Seventeen

A New Avenue To Leads And Contacts

By the time the feature appeared, we had been in business for quite a few years. During this time, most of our deals had come from going to the courthouse and using the system outlined earlier.

Once the *Post* acticle appeared, however, the phone began "ringing off the wall." Some of the calls were from people over 500 miles away.

You can imagine how surprised we were when people started calling us for advice. Some even drove up to our house to meet us personally.

Many of the callers said that they would be willing to buy land from me at a good price. This opened up a whole new avenue of important leads to pursue. It also produced some very good profits.

As a direct result of the article, one man called and said he knew of 43 acres of land for sale in a nearby county. He wanted to know if I would pay him a finder's fee of $1,000 for his information. I agreed to look at the land and get back in touch with him.

When Dianne and I drove to the acreage, we were immediately impressed. The land had good road frontage and was just two miles from a new freeway that was four years from completion. The original owners had willed one acre of land to one of their daughters and she was using her acre as a home. It had old cars and trash piled around. The clutter was everywhere. But even with its bad appearance, we realized the the new freeway would be increasing the value of the land with every month that passed. We agreed to purchase it and pay the man his $1,000 finder's fee.

There was one problem with the acreage. The administrator of the 43 acres was an elderly lady. She said there were about 15 other heirs to the property, so this meant that it would be some time before we could get everyone to agree to sign the necessary papers. She asked $550 per acre and she began the process of contacting the other heirs. This took about four months. Then the land had to be surveyed and the title brought up to date. I signed an earnest money contract with $500 dollars down and took it to a title company. During this period, I went to a local bank and asked for a 60% loan of the appraised value. The bank sent their appraiser out to the property and he appraised it at $2,000 per acre. The potential of the land was very high because of the location next to the freeway. I was able to borrow 60% of that amount, which was $1,200 per acre.

At the time of closing, the previous owners received $550 per acre and the title company wrote me a check for $27,950. In borrowing the $1,200 per acre from the bank, I had agreed to seven-year financing, paying interest for only the first two years and then interest and principle for the next five years. Since I had borrowed the money for the transaction, I did not have to pay income tax on the amount I received from the title company. You do not have to pay tax on borrowed money.

I was in no hurry to sell the land because I knew that it would be steadily increasing in value and would be increasing fast. I held the property for about 18 months and then sold it for $1,650 per acre, still well under the amount that it had been appraised by the bank officer at the time of my purchase from the original heirs—$2,000 per acre to be exact. This meant that my buyer would be able to sell it for a considerable profit if he wanted. Dianne and I grossed $47,300 on this sale.

In looking back, I remember that three months before the article appeared, I had refused to be interviewed for the story by another reporter at the same paper. At that time, I was afraid of the publicity—afraid that something would come out in the newspaper that wouldn't be right.

Now I must say that I think the reporter did an excellent job in describing my business. As a result of this experience, I would encourage you at some point in your career to share your expertise with others. Save such sharing for the right time and it will give you a boost.

Readers Comments

Dear Friends,
 It was an inspiration to talk to you recently on the phone. I have mailed out over 100 letters in the last three weeks and replies are coming in almost daily. I am still waiting for that "good deal" to come along. Meanwhile, I want your Newsletters, as I'll need all the help I can get!
 Thank you for pointing out the possibilities of a new and profitable way of life. The comments in your book about remembering the former days of poverty and not letting wealth become one's god were especially appreciated.
 Thank you for sharing this plan.

Mr. & Mrs. Rankin, Rosebud, Montana

The Reader's Page

Everybody should have his own gas well.

Chapter Eighteen
Every Texan Has A Gas Well—So I Got One, Too!

Every Texan has a gas or oil well, right?

Well, I never believed it either, but now I own one! This transaction was one of the most interesting in which I've been involved. As usual, it came about as a result of our letter campaigns.

About three months after we had sent out one of our regular blanket mailings to owners in one of our counties, we received a reply from a woman who owned 193 acres. She offered to sell the property to us at $450 an acre.

The tract in question was beautiful and had a riverside location. But there was a very sticky problem which threatened to ruin the deal. The road to the property had never been dedicated to the county. Basically, the property was landlocked. Without access to the land, even the best acreage is relatively worthless.

I undertook to find a solution to the problem. I found out who owned the property across from the tract I wanted to buy and had my attorney contact him and request an easement across his property. We suggested that the easement be dedicated to the county.

The other owner was an attorney and he agreed to our suggestion in about four days.

With the matter of access worked out, I then told the original owner that I would buy her land if we could arrange attractive terms. She was quite willing because she didn't need money in cash. We agreed on $15,000 down with 20-year financing. I was to pay 8% interest for the first 10 years only and I was to receive all the mineral rights.

We then signed the earnest money contract.

Within three weeks of the signing, the elderly lady became ill. She died before the sale was completed.

Her appointed executor fulfilled the earnest money contract. It took extra time because the deceased lady's will had to be probated. Even before the transaction had been completed, an oil company had contacted me requesting to lease the land. Since I was buying the land, I would soon be the owner of public record. Therefore it was my permission they asked to drill for gas on the property.

When the transaction first began, I did not know the gas well potential. But within two weeks after I closed the land deal, the oil company leased the property for $3,800 in cash.

After holding the property for about six months, I put an ad in the classified section of the paper, advertising the property as beautiful riverside acreage and within four days we had signed an earnest money contract for $1,125 per acre. We were paid $37,500 down and took a second lien note for $119,000 using the land as collateral. I explained to my buyer that the land was leased to an oil company and that I would give him one-fourth of the minerals and royalties and I would keep three-fourths for myself. The buyer agreed to these terms because I was offering him a good buy on the acreage itself.

In less than two years after I sold the land, the oil company had developed a good gas well on this tract. My portion of the income from the gas well is between $1,000 and $1,100 each month. This amount alone is more than I ever thought I would be making before discovering this system. All this from just one letter.

The Reader's Page

The Reader's Page

Chapter Nineteen
One Deal Leads To Another

A satisfied customer will often become a steady customer. He'll come knocking on your door again, as the next two examples will show.

One particular gentleman owned 283 acres of land that he wanted to sell at $380 per acre. We thought the property in question attractive enough to warrant this payment. The owner said he wanted cash. I went through the procedure of getting permanent financing for the transaction.

But at the last minute his financial condition changed so that he could no longer accept a cash payment. This was certainly an unusual twist.

After much discussion, I agreed to accept $35,974 from him. This was the difference between the old loan and the new loan that was now necessary because of his special tax problem. I gave him a note payable for that amount to be collected in one year. I also gave him a second lien note of $51,580.

Upon closing, I walked off with over $35,000 in my pocket for property I had just bought!

We kept the property for about six months to achieve a capital gain. Then we sold the property to a buyer who agreed to pay us $14,343 down. He also agreed to pay off the $35,974 note we owed and to assume the note for the balance.

We had grossed some $50,000 on this deal using absolutely none of our own money.

A year later, the man who had purchased the property from us sold the land at a good profit. And every individual involved in the deal was happy.

The original owner was so pleased that he contacted us for another transaction. This deal involved 320 acres of land in a nearby county that he wanted to sell at $475 per acre. The property was 60 miles from Houston and had some excellent features, including a $25,000 water well and two county roads leading to the acreage.

On this deal he needed a lot of cash to offset the amount of equity he had in the property. But he didn't want the cash immediately. We used the same technique employed in the first transaction. This time I took $17,500 and gave him a note for that amount to be collected at a specified future date. I walked out of the closing with $17,500 in cash, and I did not have to pay a penny in tax because it was borrowed money, plus I owned the land.

I kept the tract for six months before selling it for $40,000 down. The terms of my contract with the new buyer showed that he assumed all notes and obligations, including the $17,500.

Because of our letter-writing effort, we had contacted one man who was eventually responsible for our grossing a profit of over $107,000. Of course, he was well aware of the fact that we made profits on our deals with him. But he was happy because we also served his purpose.

I always like to point out these two transactions because it illustrates my theory that everyone should leave a closing happy with the outcome. In both of these deals, the original owner was happy, I was happy, and the people who were my buyers were also pleased. Everyone made a profit.

Readers Comments

Dear Mr. Stephenson:
Your book will be a landslide, I know it! One more point about your fantastic book is that you were able to put into print, so succinctly the minute consecutive chain of events which must take place to complete the legal process of land and mineral right transfer—with or without legal tender being involved.
Mrs. Kelly Smith, Oakland, California

The Reader's Page

Chapter Twenty
A Very Personal Deal

Considering the fact that we have been involved in so many land transactions, it is very difficult for me to pick one or two and say, "These are my favorites."

In the majority of our transactions, we seldom meet the people from whom we buy land. However, two of the more pleasant land deals Dianne and I made involved three sisters, all between 60 - 70 years of age. The sisters had never married. They had lived and worked together all their lives.

Dianne and I have often thought how fortunate we were that this was one of the few exceptions. This experience came fairly early in our new business careers.

As usual, we received a response from one of our many letters regarding acreage in one of our selected counties. The sisters wrote that they would like to meet with us and discuss the terms of sale. We arranged a luncheon meeting.

At the meeting, each time I tried to steer the conversation around to business matters, they turned the conversation back in the direction of friendly chitchat. Finally, after several such efforts, Dianne and I decided to just have a good time and enjoy their company. We had a very pleasant visit.

The sisters said that they would let us know the following week about the price and terms of sale. After more personal talk, the meeting broke up. We could then do nothing more than wait for them to contact us.

The next week we received a letter from them saying that they would sell the land to us at $600 an acre. They requested several specific terms which were all acceptable to us. We had a title company prepare an earnest money contract. When the sisters had returned the contract to us, we advertised to sell the property.

It didn't take long to get a buyer. We asked just $950 an acre for the property. The land sold the second day the advertisement ran, and we had a double closing to the tune of $11,000 profit.

Further research in the courthouse by Dianne revealed that the sisters owned 33 more acres. We wrote a letter asking if they wanted to sell this tract. A "yes" response came, and we agreed to their suggested selling price of $600 per acre.

While we were waiting for the transaction to close, the sisters contacted the person to whom they had been leasing the acreage. They advised him that the land was being sold.

It was reported that the man made an immediate trip to see the sisters. He offered them $800 per acre—$200 more per acre than the price we were paying. The sisters absolutely refused even to listen to the man. He had traveled some 500 miles to see them and they wouldn't open their door to hear his offer.

I believe their desire to sell us the land was a direct result of the personal contact we had established during our first transaction. The sisters told us of the man trying to persuade them to let him come in and discuss the matter. But they did not know him as they knew us and therefore wouldn't give him any consideration.

Again, the people who were involved in this transaction were happy. The sisters were happy; we were happy; and the buyer we found for our land later sold at a profit and he was happy too. (Of course, the man who had been leasing the land from the sisters was probably very unhappy!)

I would again like to stress that almost all of our transactions were a direct result of our regular letter campaigns.

For example, a California man responded to one of our letters saying that he would sell his property at $700 per acre. We talked on the telephone two or three times to work out the exact arrangements of the sale. This also gave Dianne and me an opportunity to go out and look at the property.

The 30 acres was a good piece of property. It was two miles from a major freeway and was approximately 382 feet deep and had a mile of road frontage. It appeared to be an excellent prospect for subdividing and selling in house lots. There was only one drawback. The owner didn't have any mineral rights. In my opinion, I think mineral rights are very important. I always like to keep at least one-fourth of the mineral rights to any property I sell.

We went ahead and bought the property anyway. The California owner had told us to put $500 earnest money down with a title company he knew and we did. It wasn't long before he returned the signed contract.

On this particular transaction, I decided to go through a bank for a loan. I asked for financing of 60% of the appraised value. The bank appraised the property at $2,000 an acre. I was therefore able to borrow $1,200 per acre on the property. At the time of closing, I walked away with $14,000 in cash and a note for the loan. Again, we had to pay no tax on this money because it was borrowed.

I kept the land for about 18 months and then sold two 10-acre tracts for cash at $1,750 per acre. With this money, I was able to pay off the third tract, which was then free and clear. I sold the third 10-acre tract in two-acre segments for $3,000 an acre with terms of $500 down and $150 per month. On the last 10 acres, I am carrying my own paper.

This was an excellent buy for me and for my buyers. We have all made a profit, whether we sold the land or used it for the purpose for which we bought it.

Once you get those letters in the mail, things are going to start happening. And you can rest assured that they will be positive things.

The Reader's Page

Chapter Twenty-One
A Bad Deal Turns Good

Roy Powers is a man of great ability and excellent judgment. Although still in his 30's, Roy has accumulated considerable real estate holdings in and around Houston.

I first met Roy in 1968.

Using our usual system of blanket mailings to landowners in a selected county, I had recently acquired 10 acres of land for $1,250 per acre. The market value of the property was estimated to be in the neighborhood of $2,200 - $2,400 per acre. Roy responded to our classified ad, stating that he wanted to look at the property. I told him how to get there. In two hours, he called back and said he wanted to purchase it at $1,800 per acre. We agreed to his offer and made arrangements to close the deal with a title company that he uses. He said that the earnest money contract would be ready to sign and he would have a check for us in the amount of $5,000. However, he wouldn't be there in person because he was going fishing in Mexico.

We closed this deal and deeded the property to him without ever meeting him.

About six months later, Dianne and I purchased 80 acres at $825 per acre. After visiting with a real estate man, we decided to give him an open listing on the property at $1,450 per acre. Two days later he brought me a contract for the land at $1,250 per acre; the buyer agreed to assume the financing that I had acquired from the previous owner.

The new owner was Roy Powers. Once again, at the closing he had the money down at the title company. The papers were signed and a check was waiting. And again, all we had to do was sign the deeds and necessary papers over to him.

Several weeks later I started wondering who this man was. I had sold him two pieces of land and had yet to meet him.

I called his secretary and asked for a luncheon appointment. She arranged our meeting, and the luncheon turned into a long afternoon of interesting talking and visiting. We became good friends and now get together often.

Roy is a developer of land and his drive to succeed in this area is unmatched. He specializes in subdivisions having two- to five-acre tracts. Generally he asks for a small down payment and carries his own notes. He also owns about 55 rent homes and four mobile home parks.

In 1973, Roy was considering buying 120 acres of land full of underbrush and large trees for $1,750 per acre. His payments with principle and interest would be in the neighborhood of $50,000 per year. When Roy asked my opinion on this land, I told him that the price seemed high and that he might have trouble selling it unless it was subdivided.

But Roy wasn't discouraged and he bought the land.

A few months later, Roy called and asked if I wanted to see the land as it looked now. We drove to the property and there were maintenance men and bulldozers everywhere. Streets were being put down. Roy had decided that he couldn't sell it in the condition he had purchased it, so he had decided to subdivide it into one-half acre lots for homes. He had invested a large amount of money in the improvements he had made. As he finished one section of the subdivision, he sold it. Then he would begin another section. The selling price for a one-half acre homesite was $4,950.

He had made a very successful operation out of this "bad" investment. Roy Powers is truly a remarkable self-made man.

Land continues to represent one of the most consistent and favorable opportunities in an environment of economic beginnings, land has played a vital role in the lives of many.

It is the most basic element in sustaining life itself apart from the sun's energy and the air that we breathe. Unlike these two items, however, it is also an investment opportunity.

People today are scrambling for investment opportunities that offer safety, the prospect of reasonable return and the protection from ever present inflation, in fact, one good land investment can equal a lifetime of work.

Roy Powers

another day at the ranch.

Chapter Twenty-Two
Settling Down On The Ranch

The transactions which I have mentioned in this book represent only a small portion of those in which Dianne and I have been involved. For the most part, we have accomplished them by using the very basic system I have described. Complication has not been the foundation of our success. Instead, simplicity and a strong adherence to some very basic principles are responsible for our achievements.

But don't be misled by the simplicity of our system. We have presented it in a straightforward manner because we want to emphasize that you can do the same things that we did and achieve success, too. The whole purpose in our writing this book is to give you a guideline to follow. Complicated directions only confuse the issue, so we have purposefully avoided anything that might blur your thinking.

Unlike Hughes, Hunt, Rockefeller and Hearst, our path to success is one that you can follow. This is a plan that will work today, the modern method by which you can make money. Others accomplished their success in a manner that was suitable for their time, but the way of making money in the early part of the century is not a way that will work now—at least not for most people. On the other hand, our system is still working for us right now. This is a system that *can* serve as your foundation to future financial success and security.

The facts contained in this book are just that—facts.

There is one land transaction that I have not discussed in this book that I would like to tell you now. Of all our deals, this is the one that has the most meaning for Dianne, our children and me. It is symbolic of our financial success and future security. This is the transaction in which we became owners of a 345-acre ranch.

There were two owners involved in this very important transaction. They lived out-of-state and we contacted them in our usual way—by letter. We offered them $225 per acre for the land. They accepted our cash offer and we signed an earnest money contract for $1,000.

After taking the contract to a mortgage man who specialized in ranch loans, we discovered that the acreage was landlocked—there was no road easement and therefore no access to the property.

The only man who could help me resolve the situation was the owner of the adjacent property. Unfortunately he had been involved in a disagreement with the father of the previous owner and would probably not be overly anxious to help me with the matter of obtaining access to the land.

After discovering that he was a rancher, I decided upon a plan. I approached him with the idea that once I owned the land, he could arrange to lease it. He seemed pleased at this suggestion. I told him that if he would help me secure an easement I would lease all of the property to him for grazing purposes for the first three years at $100 per year.

This was a deal he found impossible to refuse. He helped me obtain an easement and I bought the property.

An appraiser valued the property at over $750 per acre at the time I bought it for $225 per acre. Today, the property around my ranch is selling for $4,000 per acre subdivided. I could sell my ranch immediately for a profit of over $3,500 per acre on 345 acres. (Take the time to figure out the profit in that deal and then you will understand the potential wealth of your future!)

But we haven't sold the property and it's very likely that we never will. To us, this land represents more than potential profit. This ranch, even more than our beautiful home, symbolizes success and a safe future. It reminds us of the financial transformation that has taken place during the past decade. We have sentimental ties to this property and to us there is not a monetary figure that could represent success and security like the ranch itself. We have dug lakes on the land and we go hunting and fishing there with our friends. We raise registered cattle and quarterhorses. We do things together on the ranch and we share our symbol with the people who mean the most to us.

At the beginning of the book I asked you to make a list of the things that you value in life and order them according to the priority in which you want to achieve them. I said then that you shouldn't be ashamed if financial security was near the top of the list of things you value. It is a worthwhile goal. It means a new standard of living for you and your family. It will also open doors of service to your friends, your community, and your church. It will enable you to do and enjoy things that you have thought impossible up to now.

I remember running away from home when I was 16. It was frightening to be alone in the world.

I remember selling vacuum cleaners. I remember Dianne and me struggling to make ends meet with not even enough money to provide for all of the necessities. It's humbling to look back and see how far we've come.

But I also remember where I started and who I was when I started. Wealth has distorted the values of many who have obtained it. Dianne and I always remember the story that Neal Elden told about being the only man in the world. We realize the importance of things that money can't buy. Money can do many things that are good for people, but if the pursuit of money becomes your God, then you will become money's Satan.

Financial security lies before you. But remember to think about money in more than one way.

Readers Comments

Dear Dianne & Jim:
Thanks for everything. You have confirmed most of my beliefs and thinking on handling tax roll land transactions.
I must confess that when I first saw your ad, I was skeptical. I phoned a few people in the area that I was acquainted with and found one who knew you slightly. He did a little checking and called me, all enthused. Told me about your. . . . deals. You are the genuine article, all right. My warmest congratulations.
Mr. David Magee, Kerrville, Texas

Readers Comments

JIM, your book is terrific. It's worth a thousand. An amazing story, especially the Dianne part in it, a beautiful gal. I am 69, sole income is social security but I can see where my financial worries are over now from here on in—to the final whistle in the final quarter. I'm looking for a partner—so I'll be sending for your newsletter within 30 to 40 days. I'll be shooting for that million within 3 years—inevitably 2! or 1!
God Bless! Best wishes! Keep up the Good Work!
Charles E. Delmonico, Pompano Beach, Florida

I am willing to help. I will be your partner.

Chapter Twenty-Three
I'll Be Your Partner

This may well be the most important chapter of the book. It demonstrates the confidence I have in the universal system I developed and described.

If you follow the steps I outlined and combine them with a little common sense, I believe that you—or anybody—can make money buying and selling land. At this point you have enough information to make this sytem work without further general help or counsel. In selecting examples of transactions I made to illustrate my system, I tried to include a variety of situations that I had encountered to give you an idea of how to handle specific problems which are likely to confront you.

But there is no way that I can write a book to cover every situation that may develop. For this reason I have developed a service for those of you who may feel you need further guidance of a specific nature.

I will be working as a consultant to give persons starting their own ventures the benefit of my years of successful experience. In discussing your particular situation, I may tell you that you need more specific information. I can give you suggestions on how to write an advertisement for that very special deal you are about to finalize. I may give you technical information that is pertinent to your unique situation. I will provide many types of assistance on specific transactions that you may need.

For this service, I will charge you a fee of $80 per hour, with a minimum cost of $40 for 30 minutes. Considering that an hour's worth of advice might very well net you a profit of some $50,000—possibly more—my fees are not expensive.

I stressed the importance of having a professional

approach to this venture earlier, and it's appropriate to do so again at this point.

Using a professional who can give you good advice on your business deals may save a great deal of expense later on. The services of a CPA, a well-qualified land attorney, a good title company, and if you like, an experienced land dealer will benefit you in the long run. Professionals know their business. They have the knowledge to find a problem, to analyze the good and bad points of a business deal, and to give you advice on how to handle particular situations. I cannot stress this point too often.

But some of you may still be a little nervous about the idea of getting into this venture alone. Go out and find a good deal. *If you don't have the cash for the earnest money contract or you are hesitant about spending your own money, I am completely willing to become your partner in an arrangement that will fit your needs.*

Obviously, my agreeing to do this depends entirely upon my complete analysis of all the factors involved and my affirmative decision to proceed with the deal.

But I have such confidence in my system that I am willing to be your partner if you find the right kind of deal—one similar to the many I have already described. I am certain that this arrangement will be one that will make us both a profit. If I didn't have complete confidence that this system would work, I certainly wouldn't offer to enter a partnership with you. If you need my assistance, you can reach me by telephone or letter and we can discuss that deal you are thinking about and the terms that would be mutually agreeable.

But I would prefer that you take the system, go out and find a good deal, and handle the contract yourself. I want you to become financially independent without having to share any of the profits with anyone— *including me.*

I want you to make it on your own. You can make it on your own. Go on out and do it!

Good luck to you in your pursuit of financial success and security, and God Bless You.

Readers Comments

Dear Mr. Stephenson:
Received issue No. 1 of the Newsletter and am truly glad for the information that was covered. I can see right now I made a wise decision in subscribing (and you can quote me). . . .

Mr. Redd L. Long, Duluth, Minnesota

The Reader's Page

Interest

A real sharp real estate investor has to be able to figure interest in his head faster than other people can figure interest on paper.
 A quick rule of thumb is 6 x 6 = $1.00. That means 6% x $6,000 = app. $1.00 per day. 9% x $6,000 = app. $1.50 per day. 12% x $6,000 = app. $2.00 per day. You can multiply and come up with any such multiplications such as 6% x $60,000 = app. $10,00 per day. 6% x $120,000 = $20.00 per day.
 As you get used to these figures you will be able to add or subtract from any of these figures and get the approximate answer in just a second.

Examples

For interest at 6%:
    6% x $12,000 = $2.00 Per day
    6% x $18,000 = $3.00 Per day
    6% x $24,000 = $4.00 Per day
    6% x $30,000 = $5.00 Per day
    6% x $36,000 = $6.00 Per day
    6% x $42,000 = $7.00 Per day

For interest at 9%:
    9% x $12,000 = $ 3.00 Per day
    9% x $18,000 = $ 4.50 Per day
    9% x $24,000 = $ 6.00 Per day
    9% x $30,000 = $ 7.50 Per day
    9% x $36,000 = $ 9.00 Per day
    9% x $42,000 = $10.50 Per day
    9% x $48,000 = $12.00 Per day

For interest at 12%:

12% x $12,000 = $ 4.00 Per day
12% x $18,000 = $ 6.00 Per day
12% x $24,000 = $ 8.00 Per day
12% x $30,000 = $10.00 Per day
12% x $36,000 = $12.00 Per day
12% x $42,000 = $14.00 Per day
12% x $48,000 = $16.00 Per day

Dear Jim:

I have been keeping up with your newsletter inasmuch as I have land investments of my own. The suggestions for subdividing land found in Volume Two, Issue No. Three, when applied to my particular circumstances appears to be just the program I'll need to follow; and, as a matter of fact, with nominal variations, has worked for me very well in the past. Few buyers, when acquiring land in acreage of relatively large tracts, think ahead in terms of selling small portions of the tract to provide financing for the whole tract. This, of course, is very aptly pointed out in your recent newsletter in reference to planning ahead for subdivision if such becomes necessary or desirable. It's a poor time to discuss releases upon smaller portions of the tract at a time when you are ready to sell. As you pointed out, this should be considered when you are buying initially. It could be the whole difference in whether you succeed or not in this particular deal.

Having been a small part of the "coming of age" for Fort Bend County, Texas, it occurs to me, more than ever, the subtle suggestions dropped us through your newsletter are absolutely invaluable. I have been about as guilty as the next man of the phrase, "not being able to see the forest for the trees," however, as I read your newsletters, the applications of common sense appears to be about all that was lacking in part of my transactions.

With warmest personal regards to you and Dianne, I remain,

LAW OFFICES OF

MARVIN REEVES KANAK

NEEDVILLE, TEXAS - 793-6321

WEST COLUMBIA, TEXAS - 345-3253

HOUSTON, TEXAS - 224-5654

Dear Mr. and Mrs. Stephenson,

We still can't believe it, but your system of land transactions worked for us. Not just once, but twice, and with others pending.

I've got to admit, though, we came very close to not sending off for your book.

We have been married for almost 30 years. My husband has worked as an industrial insulator in a refinery for the past 31 years. He is a typical conservative, working man, and negative toward anything he could term as "easy money."

When we saw your ad and discussed your book, he reacted in his usual skeptical manner, reluctantly giving in to letting me send for it. After reading your book, we discussed our individual potentials and decided we'd try it.

I've worked in a department store for years, and having met the public and dealt with people, I felt like I had a lot to offer to this land system of yours. However, I have since quit my job, in order to allow me more time to pursue our new adventure.

My husband is off weekends which leaves him free to scout out our new land finds and show the land to our prospects. He is also good at working out flexible terms with them. Our two grown sons have become interested and are now helping us too.

We've got a lot to learn yet, and feel the tips in your newsletters are invaluable. For instance, never having invested before, we knew nothing about the savings gained through "capital gains" that your C.P.A. described. We are looking forward to the newsletter you mentioned in your book on subdividing, as we have in mind a tract of land in an area where mobile homes are popular.

If you'd like to use my letter in any way, to encourage others, you have our permission, as a token of our appreciation.

In closing, we'd like to thank both of you. You'll never know how much this new opportunity means to us.

Mr. and Mrs. D. M. Thompson, Pearland, Texas

Dear Jim & Dianne,

I'm the Executive Vice-President of a young chain of Texas-Oklahoma Consumer Credit Corporation, with thirteen branch offices and over thirty-five full time employees. At the present time we do not have any type of retirement plan. Three of my key employees will be retiring within the next five years.

After I had ordered your book several of my employees had asked to borrow it, and enjoyed it very much. So I ordered fifteen more books and distributed them among my offices, so that on week-ends and their spare time they could if they so desired, work on something to add to their financial security.

Already one of my managers has bought a home and some acreage using your system at a "super savings." Others say that the book has been very educational and hopefully they can put their newly gained knowledge to use.

J. M. Eason

Dear Jim,

Your third newsletter is just unbelievable. It showed me how to buy land at retail, subdivide it and come out w/$19,000.00 in my pocket!

All I did was follow your system just like you describe. I put up $500.00 earnest money and have made more money than I've ever had before in my life.

Keep those newsletters coming! I can't afford not to get them as soon as they come off the press!

                      Mr. Robert Schmidt, Albany, New York

Epilogue

The response that Dianne and I are getting from the publication of this book is almost unbelievable. Letters and telephone calls come in a steady stream. What do our readers say? Things like:

"Yes, Jim, I know that your system works. Three or four years ago, my uncle bought some land on the outskirts of Cincinnati. First, he found the location he wanted to buy land in. Then he found some acreage that he liked. After that, he asked a neighbor in that vicinity where the landowner lived. It turned out that the landowner lived out-of-state. Just like you and Dianne, he went to the tax rolls and looked the owner up. My uncle then wrote him a letter and ended up buying the land at half its value. He sold seven acres and doubled his money. With that money, he built a lovely home free and clear on the remaining three acres."

Many people write to tell us that they are starting to use our system and are finding that it really is very simple. For instance, we hear things like this often.

"Jim, my wife and oldest daughter have already gone to the county seat and gotten the names and addresses of over 800 landowners. This took them only a few hours of work. We will be in the process of mailing out the letters soon. Our family is very excited about this new venture."

Some of the telephone calls we get go like this.

"I can buy this tract of land way below market price. But I don't really know how to make the owner an offer. I'm afraid that I may say or do something wrong. Would you tell me, step-by-step, how to do it?"

"Jim, I'm aware of where I can buy 26 acres right now. The land was left to the owner by his parents. I know he needs to sell the land to raise money and I want to buy it. But what do I do if he has no mineral rights? Do I go to an attorney first? And then what should I do? Also, where can I get the money?

These questions are typical questions that Dianne and I were also asking when we first started. It took months, even a few years, of uncertainty and making mistakes before we learned exactly how to handle every type of situation that can arise when you are dealing in land.

But don't feel bad. The system *does* work. And it will work without any large investments. Even though we made some mistakes, we remained excited and confident about the big and good prospects that we knew the system would afford us.

In the fall of 1972, a close friend and his wife found an excellent tract containing 61 acres in the suburbs of Houston. They asked Dianne and me to help them buy this land. The owners lived out-of-state. Dianne and I helped our friends write a simple letter inquiring if the land was for sale. Like all our letters, this one was simple and to the point. Ten days later, our friends received a letter from the landowners stating that they would sell. They asked how much money per acre George and his wife would be willing to pay.

Dianne and I went with our friends to look at the land. It was a beautiful piece of property with a lot of road frontage, some brush, and a few large trees. We thought it would be good to subdivide the acreage in small tracts. By doing this, we figured that the land could be subdivided in two- to five-acre tracts for at least $4,500 per acre.

Our friends and I sat down and Dianne wrote the letter. We said that we thought we could pay around

$1,800 per acre. We would put ten thousand dollars down and the owners could carry their papers at 7-1/2% interest with a 10-year pay out on the balance.

Two weeks later, George and his wife came over. They were very excited. They had received a letter from the owners. The owners stated they were willing to sell the land at $1,800 per acre and on those terms.

But George and his wife didn't know what to do next. We sent George to our attorney, who prepared an earnest money contract and mailed it to the seller. After we received the signed earnest money contract back from the landowner, I got another idea. Dianne wrote another letter for George. In the letter, George offered to pay them $1,500 per acre cash for the land. At this stage, the landowner had already agreed to sell at $1,800 according to the earnest money contract; but on the other hand, there was a chance that a cash offer would be more appealing. He might be willing to sell for less money in order to receive cash. (Of course, before we had written this letter, I had assured George that he would have no trouble getting 100% loan on this property. There are nationwide lenders begging for good real estate loans.) As it turned out, the landowners accepted cash in a lump sum rather than a larger amount over a period of time.

George and I went down to a savings and loan association and he applied for 50% of the appraised value of the land. The association sent their appraiser to see the land, and he appraised it at $4,250 per acre. George got a 100% loan, plus he walked away from the title company with a check for approximately $36,000 as well as title to the property.

On the new loan, he got five-acre release tracts to be released from the original loan as he planned to subdivide it in five-acre tracts. After he had closed the loan on the 61 acres, he had the land surveyed in five-acre tracts. He had very little expense in getting the property ready to sell. George and his wife netted over $1,500 per acre on a 10-year pay out. This is easily the largest amount of money he had ever made.

There is a very happy ending to this story about these two fine people. Two-and-a-half years later, George took an early retirement from the City of Houston. He is now very successful and active in the real estate business as an investor. He has no real estate license and no office, but he is making large profits using our system. They send out an average of 15 or 20 letters each week to out-of-county owners. But if George and his wife had not asked Dianne and me what to do about this excellent land they wanted to buy, they might not have been able to enjoy their new life. They are finally free from financial worry.

Because Dianne and I are getting so many questions, we have decided to put out a monthly newsletter. This service to you will cost only $92.50 each year. With this service comes our years of experience, complete with a step-by-step breakdown of the many questions that you may have.

The Newsletter Will Save Time—Remember, Time IS Money

We've all heard the old saying, "Time is money." But just because this saying is old and somewhat worn doesn't make it less true for you and me today than it was for people years ago. Learning anything well requires some time, regardless of what you are learning. I've developed a special newsletter just for my readers that has been designed as a learning tool. In other words, these newsletters are written to enable you to begin your business immediately and will explain aspects that you can use as soon as you start dealing in land.

We Had Nothing But a Dream

I am glad that I had a wife with the willpower and the spunk to go ahead in a new field alone. We had no financial backing, no experience, no money—nothing but an idea. But we made it. You can make it too. Our system worked for us and it will work for you.

Do you have a friend that always seems to be getting a better job, a new car, or a new home? Or how about your boss? Does he always seem to be getting even further ahead? These are the people who dare to make important decisions.

Set Your Goals High

Set your goals high. That $92.50 per year for our newsletter and consultation will be the best investment that you have ever made. You and your family can have the same success that we had. Why? Because the business is already there. You don't have to be a big financial investor to start. This new service will not only keep you updated and give you current information. It will also provide step-by-step methods, examples, and ideas to help you in your quest for financial success. I will also answer your questions and help you find the right solutions to your particular problems via telephone or letters. This part of the service is actually what will make the difference between success and failure. There is no charge for these consultations. I will help you locate information, give you specific advice on problems that you may encounter, and possibly even act as your partner.

Be Your Own Boss

If you have set your goals high, you can't afford *not* to invest in this service. I have to assume this is already the case because you have bought this book. The system makes it easy to make money, but with this extra service and newsletter, a beginner can avoid mistakes that only experience teaches. By using the services of an experienced investor, you can turn a bad deal into a super deal. I know that I can show you how to have complete and absolute control over your financial destiny. Your $92.50 per year is only 25¢ per day—a minimum investment considering that your financial success and security is at stake. This is probably the best 25¢ a day that you will ever spend.

Make That Decision Today

Land is also the best hedge against inflation. It is the only thing I know of that increases faster than money decreases. The future has never looked brighter for any kind of property. There is now a massive movement across the entire United States. People are moving to the suburbs to get away from problems in the inner city and for better schools for their children. People are buying one or more acres, building a home, and commuting to work inside the city limits. Needless to say, there is a fortune to be made in land anywhere in the United States. Just use our system.

Some of the step-by-step advice in our newsletter will be:

1. How to locate land.
2. How to write the owners and arrive at a price that you can make money on.
3. How to write an earnest money contract.
4. How to delay the closing on purchasing land to give you maximum leverage.
5. What to do if you have no minerals.
6. How to sell or borrow on your earnest money contract.
7. What to do if there is a title problem and how to solve it.
8. What to do on property where you can only buy out a portion of owners who hold an undivided interest in a tract of land.
9. How to negotiate for better bargains.
10. Should a tract of land be sold as a single piece of property or should it be sold in subdivided

tracts? Which way is the method to make a bigger profit?
11. Do I need a partner?
12. How to get investors to put up all the money after you have the property tied up, and still control the property with none of your own money in it.
13. How to decide when to keep property for your own personal use.
14. How to get permanent financing.
15. When should I move from part-time to full-time operations?
16. Other specific questions that you may have will be answered.

Successful People Are Decisive

One thing you should remember. Age, education and sex make no difference to your success. Consider a popular current figure.

This particular gentleman was 65 years old and on the verge of bankruptcy. At his age, he was ready for an old-age pension. But even though he was facing hopeless odds, he took his dream and turned it into a national financial landmark. What did he do? He took his now-famous product and put it in the back of his old station wagon. Then he took his product to restaurant after restaurant and asked them to use his system of cooking. Using what he learned, he established an extremely successful fast-foods chain. I greatly admire this man. Who is he? Octegenarian Colonel Harland Sanders—of Kentucky Fried Chicken fame. He thought positively and didn't let the odds bother him. He just went ahead with his plan and succeeded. Just like you will do.

Do something positive now. You owe it to yourself and your family. Let our experience work for you. At only 25¢ a day, can you afford not? We think not.

Land is one of the few effective investment opportunities that offer a place to the small investor with a bit of entrepreneurial flair. The promise of profits that real estate (and land in particular) holds out to the investor is summed up by a number of well-known figures of American history:

THEODORE ROOSEVELT: Every person who invests in well-selected real estate in a growing section of a prosperous community adopts the surest and safest method of becoming independent, for real estate is the basis of wealth.

HETTY GREEN: Real estate is an imperishable asset, increasing in value. It is the most solid security that human ingenuity has devised. It is collateral to be preferred above all others, and the safest means of investing money.

ANDREW CARNEGIE: Ninety percent of all millionaires become so through owning real estate. More money has been made in real estate than in all industrial investments. The wise young man or wage earner of today invests his money in real estate.

JOHN D. ROCKEFELLER: The fortunes of the future will be made in real estate.

FRANKLIN D. ROOSEVELT: Real estate cannot be lost or stolen, nor can it be carried away. Managed with reasonable care, it is about the safest investment in the world.

MARSHALL FIELD: Buying real estate is not only the best way, the quickest way, and the safest way, but the only way to become wealthy.

Have the Courage to Make a Decision

I feel about 60% of the people who receive this book will not act on our offer even though it is made at such a low price. Why? Because that 60% don't want to make an important decision that could affect their entire future. The individual who acts and dares to make an important decision now and not tomorrow is the one who will make the millions.

If you have never invested in land, it's time to start. The fundamentals are straightforward and easy to understand with a little study. This book is dedicated to providing insight in this regard and making clear the basic principles necessary to equip those who are motivated to plunge into the fascinating reality of land investment. **Make that decision now.**

Fill in the coupon below and mail with a check or money order payable to **Stephenson Investments**.

Mail to:
Stephenson Investments
204 South 3rd Street
Richmond, Texas 77469

Name _____

Address _____

City _____ State _____ Zip _____

Here is $92.50 for one year's subscription to the Universal System of Land Transactions Newsletter.

_____
(Signature)

Glossary of Real Estate Terms

ABSTRACT OF TITLE: A condensed summary or synopsis of a title to a parcel of real estate, showing the original and subsequent conveyances, mortgages, and all recorded documents pertaining to the title.

ACCELERATOR CLAUSE: A clause in contract, mortgage, or lease that calls for an entire balance to be due and payable immediately if any payment is overdue. It also gives the one who borrows money the right to pay more than the regular payments, or to pay the full amount prior to the maturity date without penalty.

ACCESS RIGHT: The right an owner has to enter onto and exit from his property by street, by right of way, by easement, or by other means.

ADMINISTRATOR: A person appointed by a court to settle the estate of a deceased person who left no will. (see Intestate) A deceased person who left a will would have appointed his own person, an executor (or executive), to carry out his instructions.

ADVERSE POSSESSION: A way of acquiring title to property without a deed, by making a claim and meeting certain statuatory requirements. The law allows an occupant of land who maintains "actual, open, notorious, exclusive and continuous occupancy of property" for a specific statuatory period, the right to legal title of the same property. Basically, this law serves as the statute of limitations for a legal owner who has either abandoned or "remained silent" during a statutory time from later claiming title to the property. The process is similar for easements. (See Easement by prescription.)

AFFIDAVIT OF TITLE: A sworn written statement by a seller declaring that he owns the property in question, that no one made any claim to it, and that there are no liens or judgments against him.

AGREEMENT OF SALE: A written agreement whereby a purchaser agrees to buy and a seller agrees to sell certain properties under specific terms and conditions.

BALLOON CLAUSE: Pertains to the paying off of a debt in small installments; at maturity, the remaining bulk sum is due. (It's like paying the down-payment at the end of an installment term.) The balloon clause is used in cases where monthly mortgage payments in, say, a ten-year mortgage would be prohibitive. So the mortgage is extended perhaps to 20 years, thus allowing smaller payments; but after the first ten years, the remaining sum will be paid in bulk.

CLOSING: Usually refers to the date when a buyer takes title to property, but the term closing is also used by a broker to mean the end of a particular state of negotiations where a buyer is ready, willing, and able to sign a contract.

COMMUNITY PROPERTY: Property that is accumulated by both husband and wife. Logically enough, if the property is not community property—if it was acquired independently by either party before marriage—it is called separate property.

EARNEST MONEY: The down payment given with a binder agreement showing good faith that a person is "ready, willing, and able" to purchase property or is willing to perform a certain act.

ESCAPE CLAUSE: A clause in a contract that frees a party from certain responsibilities under very specific circumstances. It is usually used when a buyer is not sure whether he can secure a VA or FHA mortgage request is disapproved. This clause is usually for the buyer's benefit.

LAND SURVEY: As all parcels of land must have definite and indisputable boundaries and identifications, it is necessary to physically chart (survey) the land to get its accurate boundaries. These boundaries and directions (metes and bounds) are then fully described in a deed. A land description must contain a beginning point, definite corners, specific lengths, specific directions, and an area measurement in accepted units (usually acres, square feet or square miles).

LIEN: A notice that is recorded signifying a debt on the property. If the debt is not satisfied, the debtor has the right through legal processes to foreclose the property. A lien can be general (against all the properties of one owner in a particular county), or specific (on only one parcel of property). All liens are good for one year and must be renewed in successive years.

RIGHT OF WAY: Simply, an easement; the right to cross another's property.

TITLE INSURANCE: An insurance policy which guarantees that, if for any reason the title should have a defect or prove to be defective, the holder will receive just compensation. Before title insurance is granted, a title search is required.

"WITHOUT RECOURSE": Words in a contract that protect a future owner of real property from any personal liability in the event of non-payment.